Hot, Sweet & Sticky

12 Romantic Feasts to Tempt Your Lover

Doreen Garrett

Prima Publishing

Published by Prima Publishing, Roseville, California. Member of the Crown Publishing Group, a division of Random House, Inc., New York.

PRIMA PUBLISHING and colophon are trademarks of Random House, Inc., registered with the United States Patent and Trademark Office.

"Moroccan Chicken with Olives and Preserved Lemons" adapted from Paula Wolfert, *Couscous and Other Good Food from Morocco*. New York: Harper & Row, 1973. Reprinted with permission of HarperCollins.

"'Until the Real Thing Comes Along' Balsamico" adapted from Molly O'Neill, "Magic Potions That Stir Food to Life," *New York Times*, 17 February 1999, p. B10. Reprinted with permission of the *New York Times*.

"Double-Delight Chocolate Pudding Cake" adapted with permission from Belmont Conference Center, Elkridge, MD; site of a "death by chocolate" conference.

"Pear Champagne" reprinted from *Café des Artistes: An Insider's Look at the Famed Restaurant and Its Cuisine* by Fred Feretti. New York: Lebhar-Friedman Books, 2000. Reprinted with permission of Lebhar-Friedman Books and Café des Artistes.

Interior design by Melanie Haage

Library of Congress Cataloging-in-Publication Data
Garrett, Doreen.
Hot, sweet, and sticky : 12 romantic feasts to tempt your lover / Doreen Garrett
p.   cm.
Includes index.
ISBN 0-7615-2967-5
1. Aphrodisiac cookery. I. Title.

TX652.S343   2002

641.5'63—dc21   2002032371

03 04 05 06 AA 10 9 8 7 6 5 4 3 2 1
Printed in the United States of America

First Edition

Visit us online at www.primapublishing.com

Contents

Acknowledgments

I would like to thank my agent, Martha Casselman—without whom there would be no first step—for her wit, hospitality, and sage advice; my parents, Arthur and Joan, for their steadfast love and support; my siblings, Andrew, Douglas, Justin, and Laura, for their encouragement (despite my early efforts in the kitchen); Frank, my compass and guide in good faith in all things; Susie, my spiritual kin; Suzanne, for her unstinting enthusiasm; editor Jennifer Basye Sander, for her belief and ideas; Maggie, for her ready and inventive help in the kitchen; the chefs who so generously provided their recipes; the friends whose scaffold of community sustains; and Brian, for the gift of his original self and for keeping me surprised.

Introduction

This is not a book for the fainthearted. But then neither is sex. That doesn't mean you need to try any of the more extreme recipes, potions, and strange ingredients that I came across while concocting these love feasts: leopard's marrow, suckling pig stuffed with eel, blood from a freshly decapitated rattlesnake, powdered rhino horn, sea turtle eggs, deer semen, marmalade of carnations, sparrow's brains, the legendary Spanish fly, various Viagras of the *Kama Sutra* and traditional Chinese medicine (such as toad skin), or any of the repugnant, highly toxic, even lethal, ointments with which a man is advised to anoint his penis before sex. As recently as 1943 an English company used an ancient Arabian prescription as the basis for a penile cream.

What it does mean is that to use the recipes in this book, you will need to harness your sense of adventure and put your heart into preparing a meal. Love is about adventure; seduction requires nothing less. Recipes are, with their orderly chronology and measurements, the bane of the real cook. Cooking by the book, one feels restrained, inhibited—it's like trying to conduct a love affair according to "The Rules." So take these recipes as guideposts and feel free to

add, omit, or substitute however your taste buds—and the situation—dictate. (Note that all recipes in this book make enough food for two servings unless noted otherwise in the recipe itself.)

So what makes a food sexy? Looks, for one thing. Ginger and asparagus gained their fame as aphrodisiacs from their resemblance to the phallus, while oysters, avocados, and coco-de-mer (the world's largest fruit) are likely considered love aids because they resemble the female sex organ. Then there's the fig, whose form evokes both sexes. In addition to appearance, foods that are rare, expensive, or forbidden have also long been considered aphrodisiacs.

And any advocate of aphrodisiacs would undoubtedly tell you that the elements of imagination, mystery, and surprise are what endow food with the power to lure a beloved or to charge one's libido. Although many aphrodisiac substances may have become commonplace and therefore less alluring, they are nonetheless powerful for their ability to act on our senses, taste buds, and memories.

Since before Aphrodite, the Greek goddess of love, sprang forth from *aphros* (sea foam) in a seashell, as famously depicted by Botticelli, people have recognized the marriage of food and sex as a natural, and necessary, act of communion and have known that the two are inseparably bound. More secular than sacred, the pillow talk that focuses on the desire to nibble on a lover's ear or "eat you up" appears in every culture.

One of the earliest love potions was Sumerian. Men mixed fat from holy cows and milk in a ceremonial bowl and anointed the

breast of a young girl, who would then willingly follow them. In the ancient Mediterranean and Near East, the liver was considered the seat of all passion and ritually consumed.

Greeks and Romans used animal parts and organs to make love potions that enhanced sexual vigor at orgies, at which there was evidently much nude frolicking, as documented in paintings and woodcuts of the time. Some of the Roman feasts were ludicrous in their lavishness. Remember the sexual high jinks in Fellini's film *Satyricon*, which comes from the Roman writer Petronius's satire of the same name? Rome's legendary decadence and use of aphrodisiac foods are described in the *Deipnosophists*, written in about 300 B.C.: "Among the presents which the Indian king Sandrocottus sent to Seleucus there were aphrodisiacs so potent when placed under the feet of lovers they caused, in some, ejaculations like those of birds."

The Hindu attitude is reflected in voluminous texts devoted to the importance of lovemaking and its essential role in everyday life, culminating in the love manual, the *Kama Sutra*. This book, a time-tested how-to on sexual and sensual pleasure according to Hindu law, values love over desire or passion and repeatedly emphasizes that lovers need only be guided by their own best instincts. Some of the recipes in this classic text are still worth trying.

The Arabs believed that stimulation of all the senses was essential for satisfying sex, and they carefully outlined how to do it in books such as *The Perfumed Garden*.

Chinese potions tended to be the most outrageous, and Chinese herbalists carefully guarded their secret recipes, which often contained lethal ingredients, for sexual alchemy.

The Christian ritual of the Eucharist, in which Christ is symbolically consumed, didn't come along until the fourth century. Before that, there was the *agape*, or love feast, in which men and women experienced a non–gender–specific (come one, come all) ecstasy. Greeks, Arabs, Africans, early Christians practicing *agape*—all these cultures and creeds believed in the power of aphrodisiacs.

Science still can't explain the power of aphrodisiacs, and some scientists contend that there's no factual basis for foods that have been touted for centuries as libido–chargers. Yet cultures separated by oceans and mountains, long before trade routes and migration enabled them to share information, selected the very same sensual foods to stimulate mental and physical responses. Who can deny that the red juiciness of a ripe tomato or strawberry, the musty scent of wild mushrooms, the salty flavor and firm flesh of lobster stimulate our senses *and* our organs?

As soon as science concedes there is some truth to an aphrodisiac formula, it changes its mind the following week in favor of some new Viagra. Just how sexy is a pill in a plastic bottle, removed from context and foreplay?

The real power of seduction lies in a meal lovingly prepared and creatively presented. It lies in recognizing that the alluring aromas, voluptuous textures, and tantalizing tastes of real food prepared with love enhance any meal's ability to entice, persuade—and seduce. The food in this book is intended to satisfy more than one kind of appetite.

Love and cooking both owe a great deal to alchemy: that intangible spritz that ignites a relationship and turns a couple of raw ingredients into something sublime on the tongue. Ever notice that when you're putting on a show or trying too hard or your heart isn't in the cooking, a dish doesn't turn out right? Cooking in a restaurant is about technique, precision, and repetition, but cooking at home is about what the Italians call "having a hand"—you have to have your hand as well as your heart in the pot. If you aren't passionately involved with a dish it will be evident.

Food is a magnet for cultural, and sexual, expression. Every day we are drawn to the table and to it we bring our preconceptions, our curiosity, our need for nourishment. Recipes are stories we tell ourselves and the lovers, family, and friends who gather around our table.

This book's culinary lexicon includes lamb and lobster, salmon, oysters, chocolate, red fruits—all foods that one normally associates with the exotic and erotic. There are also fava beans, squash flowers, and quince—delicacies once as rare to the common table as aphrodisiac foods of old. But if you're reading a cookbook that doesn't contain introductions to new foods and exciting ways of preparing them, why bother? Love itself is about the new.

Many years ago, at the beginning of our relationship, I asked my companion, "What do you want?"

"To be surprised," he answered.

So go ahead, be brave. If you're not going to go into the kitchen to win and to woo, magic just won't happen. Timidity won't do. Don't think that these foods are only properly transformed in the hands of chefs. Remember, the ultimate G–spot, or orgasm button, is the one in the brain; the way the olfactories act on the brain is one of the most primal things about us. Surprise, titillate, and intrigue your lover. The pleasure lies in improvising.

Bring more than your appetite to the table, the bed, the pasture, or wherever you choose to consume your love–food. Make your own sacrifice to the gods: Offer up your curiosity, your heart, your best "hand" in the kitchen to your love (or the one you're attempting to seduce) and to those you love. May we all feast on more delicious meals and love at all our tables.

Keep in mind and heart the French saying

L'appétit vient en mangent (eating whets the appetite)

and the Italian

Amate, amate, tutto il resto é nulla (love, love, nothing else matters).

Buon appetito e bon amore!

1

First Seductions

★ Bittersweet Chocolate Truffles ★
★ Artichokes with Orange Vinaigrette ★
★ Prosciutto-Wrapped Figs
with Balsamico ★
★ Tuna Tartare with Caviar and
Wasabi Crème Fraîche ★
★ Beef Crostini ★
★ Frico ★
★ Vanilla Breasts ★

he seduction . . . you want a series of seductive starters: a nibble of various flavors, textures, and colors that create an intriguing and varied tableau. If this is your first meal together, remember that you are telling a story, beginning what could be the most significant relationship of your life, and that this is the first chapter.

But first there is *the prelude* . . .

Bittersweet Chocolate Truffles

Makes 10 to 12 truffles

*Think of it as foreplay. Initiate the seduction with bittersweet chocolate truf-
fles and an invitation—call it a chocolate calling card. Are you still hanging
on to those black fishnet stockings? Cut them into little squares and wrap
your chocolates in them. Or cup the chocolates in a velvety rose petal. Make
your own Baci-type chocolates: Handwrite sentimental or provocative say-
ings in the language of your choice, slip one under each chocolate, and offer
to provide a translation at your drinks rendezvous. Try* Sono impazzito di te
(Italian for "I'm crazy for you").

> 10 ounces bittersweet chocolate, chopped, the best quality
>   you can find
> 2 tablespoons unsalted butter
> 3 tablespoons heavy cream
> ½ cup crème fraîche or sour cream
> ½ cup dark rum
> 2 tablespoons cocoa powder or finely chopped candied
>   ginger
> 10 to 12 paper candy cups, large rose petals, or other
>   imaginative wrappers

FIRST SEDUCTIONS

In a metal bowl set over a pot of simmering water, melt together chocolate and butter, then add heavy cream, crème fraîche or sour cream, and rum; gently whisk until smooth. Do not allow water in pot to boil. Pour mixture into a shallow metal pan, cover with wax paper, and chill thoroughly.

When the mixture is firm, put unsweetened cocoa on wax paper. Line up candy cups. Working quickly, roll about a table-spoon of chocolate mixture between your palms to make a ball, then roll the truffle in the cocoa and place in the candy cup or other wrapper. You can use a small ice cream scoop instead of your hands to shape the truffles, but I prefer the handmade look.

Artichokes with Orange Vinaigrette

The artichoke is as teasing and seductive as that hard-to-get guy or gal: Undress it, peeling back the thorny leaves to reveal the tender, tasty heart within. If the artichoke could undress itself, it would be a striptease.

Touted for centuries as an aphrodisiac, the artichoke is on the long list of foods that Catherine de Medici introduced to France. Since then, Parisian street vendors have been known to suggestively sell the thorny choke with cries of

> *Artichokes! Artichokes!*
> *Heats the body and the spirit.*
> *Heats the genitals too!*

The artichoke is an aesthetically pleasing and intriguing object: In Italian markets young spring artichokes sport purple blushes with sage and gray highlights on their leaves. The flowers of the artichoke are a wonder of vivid periwinkle purple spikes that last for weeks and make a stunning and unusual gift for your beloved.

½ lemon
8 baby artichokes
2 tablespoons olive oil
Salt and pepper
1 clove garlic, minced
¼ cup dry white wine
Orange vinaigrette (recipe follows)

Fill a medium-size bowl with cold water and squeeze in the juice from the half lemon; then add the lemon half itself.

Prepare the artichokes: Cut off about ¾ inch from the top and the ends of stems, and then break off the outer leaves. Trim off any bottom part of leaves with a vegetable peeler or knife until only pale green and yellow leaves remain. (Be ruthless here: You don't want your beloved gnawing on the tough, thorny parts instead of soft, succulent leaves.) Yes, you're discarding a lot of the vegetable, but it's worth it. As you clean the artichokes, add them to the bowl of lemon water.

Heat a sauté pan to medium heat, and add the olive oil. When it is hot, shake excess water off the artichokes and sauté for about 3 minutes. Sprinkle with salt and pepper. Add garlic and wine, and sauté until artichokes start to turn slightly brown and are tender when pierced with a fork, about 7 minutes.

Place artichokes in a bowl with the orange vinaigrette, toss, and let sit until artichokes cool to room temperature. The artichokes can also be prepared up to 1 day in advance and refrigerated.

Orange Vinaigrette

1 tablespoon balsamic vinegar
¼ cup fresh orange juice
1 tablespoon extra-virgin olive oil
½ teaspoon orange zest
4 sprigs fresh thyme
Salt and pepper

Pour balsamic vinegar in a small bowl, then whisk in orange juice. Whisk in olive oil, orange zest, and thyme. Season to taste with salt and pepper.

Suggested wine: champagne or other sparkling wine

Ode to an Artichoke

The tender—
hearted artichoke
dressed in its armor,
built its modest cupola
and stood
erect,
impenetrable
beneath
a lamina of leaves,
ruffling their leaves,
contrived
creepers, cattails,
bulbs and tubers to astound;
beneath the ground
slept
the red-whiskered carrot;
above, the grapevine
dried its runners,
the cabbage preened itself,
arranging its flounces;
oregano
perfumed the world,
while the gentle
artichoke
stood proudly in the garden
burnished
to a pomegranate glow . . .

—Pablo Neruda

From *Selected Odes of Pablo Neruda*, translator/editor Margaret Sayers Peden (Berkeley: University of California Press, 1990). Reprinted with permission.

Prosciutto-Wrapped Figs with Balsamico

Is there a more seductive and suggestive fruit? The fig leaf has appeared in Western art for centuries, and the fig is yet another of those fruits for which some believe the apple was mistaken in the Garden of Eden. "A fig it was in Eden, and a fig I say it is!" my friend Victor's Sephardic-Guatemalan mother proclaimed.

There is no uncertainty, however, about the fact that the fig dates as far back as the date and that it has been associated with rebirth, fertility, and divinities in many cultures and sects. Ancient Grecian priests had the task of "revealing the fig," or predicting the date of the figs' ripening, and scheduling appropriate rituals and festivities to celebrate their fruition.

The fig tree in my yard (which I call the mother of all fig trees, because it must be 25 feet wide) has two harvests—July and October. It's hard to wait, but to me figs are best when their soft interior turns slightly jammy and their ripe, succulent fruit give just enough to the touch (I definitely see why the Arabs still sometimes refer to testicles as figs). We are suddenly blessed with a mountain of ripe fruit that begs—and is never refused—to be eaten.

These figs can also be threaded on skewers and grilled outdoors, but take care not to overstuff them.

2 heaping tablespoons mascarpone cheese
2 teaspoons blue cheese, room temperature
8 black mission or green figs
8 walnut halves or larger pieces
8 thin slices prosciutto
Balsamic vinegar

Turn on broiler or grill. Mix the mascarpone with the blue cheese and set aside.

Wash and dry figs. Split them open down to the stem but don't cut through. Stuff each fig with the cheese mixture and then a walnut. Wrap each fig in a prosciutto slice.

Place figs on a baking sheet and broil until prosciutto starts to cook and turn brown and the cheese is melted. Remove from oven, cool to room temperature, and drizzle a tiny bit of vinegar on top of each fig.

Feed your lover these succulent stuffed figs with your fingers.

Suggested wine: riesling

Tuna Tartare with Caviar and Wasabi Crème Fraîche

Whether straight-up, fruit flavored, or chocolate, martinis are all the rage. Offer your sweetheart a more substantial variation: fresh, glistening tuna presented in a martini glass. The wasabi may make your heart skip a beat.

¼ pound sushi-grade tuna, extremely fresh, diced into
    ¼-inch pieces
¼ teaspoon extra-virgin olive oil
¼ teaspoon finely minced ginger
¼ teaspoon finely grated lemon zest
¼ teaspoon black sesame seeds
¼ teaspoon snipped chives
4 drops pure sesame oil
Squeeze of lemon juice
Salt and freshly ground black pepper
Wasabi crème fraîche (recipe follows)
1 ounce Beluga or Osetra caviar, the best quality you can find
Chive spears
3 slices challah bread or brioche, crusts trimmed, each slice
    cut into 4 triangles
4 lemon wedges

Chill two martini glasses. In a bowl combine tuna, olive oil, ginger, lemon zest, sesame seeds, snipped chives, sesame oil, lemon juice, and salt and pepper to taste. Chill, covered, for about 30 minutes.

Spoon about a teaspoon of wasabi crème fraîche into each martini glass. Mound over with half the tuna. Top with half an ounce of caviar, add a touch more crème fraîche, and garnish with chives. Toast bread triangles, and serve the tartare with toast and lemon wedges. Use a mother–of–pearl spoon or other nonreactive utensil to scoop tuna and caviar onto warm toast wedges.

Enjoy with icy dry sake, chilled vodka, or champagne.

Wasabi Crème Fraîche

2 teaspoons wasabi powder
2 teaspoons water
⅓ cup crème fraîche or sour cream
Pinch of sugar
Pinch of salt, or to taste
Squeeze of lemon juice

In a small bowl combine wasabi powder with water until completely moistened. Add remaining ingredients and whisk very well. Add a little water to achieve required consistency: It should fall from the spoon but not be too runny.

Beef Crostini

The power of horseradish is referred to in Greek mythology: Apollo was told by the Delphic oracle that the root was worth its weight in gold. Not surprisingly, given its peppery bite, horseradish is on the aphrodisiac roster, but thankfully it is not on the endangered species list, as are many other aphrodisiacs.

You may never have seen fresh horseradish, and if you can't find it, commercial is acceptable. But fresh horseradish is superior to the jarred, and it takes but a minute, using a ginger grater or the finest grater you have, to grate a tablespoon or two.

Horseradish looks like a long thick stick with a gnarly coating. It can't help but put you in mind of the kind of thing I came across a few years ago in Singapore in a Chinese "diagnostic" restaurant. The maître d' seats you and, before you order, takes your pulse, looks at your tongue, and "diagnoses" what you should eat. After dinner we were persuaded to try an odd-looking and odd-tasting drink with what appeared to be bits of fur floating in it. "Deer penis," the maître d' said, banging what looked like a bone on the table. "Make you hard like this!" he promised my companion. Whatever it was, the "deer penis" looked just like horseradish.

¼ pound beef fillet
2 tablespoons freshly grated horseradish
¼ cup crème fraîche (optional)
8 slices good-quality baguette

Heat oven to 350 degrees. Place fillet on a baking sheet and bake for 10 minutes, until beef is rare. Do not overcook. After 10 minutes, remove beef from oven and let it rest for 5 minutes.

While beef is cooking, mix the horseradish with crème fraîche if desired.

Heat broiler and place baguette slices on a baking sheet under broiler until tops are just lightly browned. Turn and repeat on other side. Spread with horseradish or horseradish cream.

Slice meat as thinly as possible, on the diagonal, and place atop crostini.

Suggested wine: gamay or cabernet franc

> *You can also try this Santerian voodoo love recipe for beef:*
> *Prepare a hamburger patty. Steep it in your own sweat. Serve it to the person desired.*

Frico

Frico *is the name of a traditional dish stuffed with onions and potatoes from Friuli, the northeast Italian region bordering Slovenia. It has also come to mean a sort of Parmesan waffle, which can be twisted into a taco and topped with a complementary fruit, such as pears or Asian pear. Valentino Restaurant in Santa Monica greets diners with a lovely flat version of this Parmesan tuile.*

In the spirit of foods both natural and prepared that are used to describe parts of male and female sexual anatomy, I think of this lovely, lacy, tasty delicacy as an apt representative of the female.

2 teaspoons flour
½ cup thickly grated fresh Parmesan cheese
1 pear or Asian pear, peeled, cored, and thinly sliced
Few leaves of mint or basil
Few drops of balsamic vinegar, the best you can afford

Heat a medium-size nonstick frying pan (a nonstick frying pan is a must) to medium-low temperature. Dust the pan with 1 teaspoon of the flour to uniformly cover the pan's surface, and then sprinkle ¼ cup of the cheese in the pan so that it forms a roughly even layer. Cook, using a wooden spoon or spatula to keep the cheese from sticking, until the frico begins to brown and bubble and form a lacy pattern, 3 to 4 minutes. Flip it to the other side to finish cooking.

Remove the cheese in one sheet from the pan, and wrap it around the spoon part of a wooden spoon so that it forms a taco-like shape. Wrap in a paper towel to absorb excess fat and set aside. Repeat to cook the second frico.

Thinly slice the pear and insert into fricos, along with the mint, and then drizzle a drop of balsamic vinegar over the top. Serve immediately.

Note: Unfilled, the fricos can be kept in an airtight container for up to 1 day.

Suggested wine: rosé

Vanilla Breasts

Makes 20 to 24 cookies

One of the delights of Sicilian pastry is its many varieties and whimsical forms. Outstanding among them is a simple shortbread-type cookie called, among a host of provocative names, Nun's Nipples, Virgin's Nipples, or Novice's Bosom. This variation on that theme is a shortbread-type walnut cookie given to me by my friend Murray, who used to run a major baking company. There are renditions of this sweet without the cherry nipple or chocolate, but they are only half the fun.

⅔ cup sugar
1 cup unsalted butter, room temperature
2 teaspoons vanilla extract
2½ cups flour
1 cup walnuts, shelled and halved
1 teaspoon baking powder
¼ teaspoon salt
20 to 24 chocolate chips or halved pieces of candied cherry

Preheat oven to 350 degrees.

Cream together the sugar and butter in a mixer for 4 to 5 min–utes. Mix in the vanilla.

Take about one third of the flour and blend it with the walnuts in a food processor, using the pulse button.

Add this mixture, the rest of the flour, and the baking powder and salt to the other ingredients in the mixer and blend until well mixed.

Using a small ice cream scoop, drop cookies onto a greased or parchment–lined baking sheet. Press a chocolate chip or candied cherry half into the top center of each cookie. Bake until cookies are lightly browned on top, 20 to 25 minutes.

Cool completely before serving. Freeze some of the cookies for a last–minute sweet when you need one.

Note: To make Chocolate Breasts, use an extra 3 tablespoons sugar and add $^{1}/_{3}$ cup unsweetened cocoa to the cookie dough at the same time you mix in the baking powder and salt.

Culinary Quickie

Chocolate

Chocolate contains caffeine, which revs us up; magnesium, which calms us down; endorphins, which jolly us up; and PEA, or phenylethylamine, a substance found in the systems of the love-giddy. It is linked to HDL, the good cholesterol, and possesses a divinely creamy texture and deeply sweet taste. What isn't winsome about such a dark and delicious treat?

In surveys of cravings, chocolate is the most frequently cited food. It is hypothesized that women crave chocolate more than men do, although I know few men who will turn it down. Personally, I find a little dark chocolate every day, better yet if consumed with red wine, keeps the libido revved up.

Chocolate was in use as far back as 600 B.C., it was recently reported in *Nature* magazine. The Aztecs and Mayans fetishized it, celebrating the cocoa bean harvest with orgies and ceremonies. Is it true that Montezuma, the Aztec emperor, drank fifty cups of hot chocolate a day in order to satisfy more than six hundred wives? Perhaps not, but the story says a lot about chocolate's ancient reputation as an aphrodisiac. These ancient peoples combined chocolate with honey or blue vanilla; their chocolates were variously pink, orange, black, or white and served mainly as a drink. But the Aztec stroke of genius was in combining this sensuous stimulant with another potent stimulating substance, chile: *voilà*, the birth of mole.

When Casanova wasn't slurping oysters and hitting on some young thing, he was partaking of the dark, delicious stuff. This was one instance when Casanova and his countryfolk agreed on substance abuse: The latter considered chocolate a powerful intoxicant and enjoyed the illicit thrill of consuming it.

Chocolate melts at human body temperature, so it needs little coaxing to soften up your sweetheart. Think of this renowned aphrodisiac as an easy dip for fruit, ice cream, or fritters.

Quick Chocolate Sauce

¼ pound chocolate, coarsely chopped
1 scant teaspoon cream

Combine chocolate and cream and melt slowly over a double boiler or in the microwave. Let cool slightly and use as a dip or sauce.

Chocolate . . . t'will make Old Women Young
  and Fresh
Create new Motions of the Flesh
and cause them to long for you-know-what
if they but taste CHO-CO-LATE!

–William Wadsworth

2

Chef's Love Menu

It's been a few weeks, you've had a few dates, so now how do you move things along? Pull out all the stops. Ratchet up the heat on the relationship by using star–studded recipes from some of America's finest chefs.

Oyster and Passion Fruit Shooters

ostriche con frutti della passiflora

from Luciano Pellegrini, chef, Valentino Las Vegas

Makes 12 shots

Demanding critics can't get enough of Piero Selvaggio's flagship Los Angeles restaurant, Valentino. Ruth Reichl named it "America's best restaurant," and R. W. Apple, Jr., has called it "the best Italian restaurant in the country," and "no one tops Piero Selvaggio as a host" (both in the New York Times).

Indeed, Selvaggio is the Baryshnikov of restaurateurs—compact, subtle, elegant, and charming. He loves wine so much that his Web site is www .welovewine.com. At Selvaggio's second Valentino, in Las Vegas's Venetian hotel, Luciano Pellegrini puts his own spin on the classic and imaginative dishes that have won the original Valentino first place in every major American restaurant and wine-list competition.

Starting the meal with this kind of sizzle can't help but ignite a relationship or make one last—even in Las Vegas. Pellegrini says, "Bottoms up: Let this titillating bite get you into the right mood, then continue playing in the kitchen. . . ." I would only add that these oyster and passion fruit shooters, so simple, daring, and erotic, issue a challenge to the meal to come: "Top this!"

6 oysters, medium size
3 passion fruits
1 tablespoon extra-virgin olive oil

Shuck oysters and keep chilled. Cut each passion fruit in half, scoop out pulp and seeds, then strain juice. Mix olive oil and passion fruit juice in blender for 30 seconds. Divide mixture into six chilled shot glasses (or you can refill glasses as they're emptied), then slide one oyster into each glass.

Suggested wine: champagne or other sparkling wine

I had a dozen oysters last night and only ten of them worked.

—Anonymous

Maine Lobster and Fava Bean Salad

from Jonathan Waxman, chef-owner, Washington Park

Jonathan Waxman is a formerly peripatetic chef who changed the face of eating in the United States with restaurants such as Jams, which effortlessly blended California cool with inventive and sophisticated Manhattan cuisine. What makes his food romantic is its gutsy earthiness; what makes his story romantic is its happy ending. After a number of consulting gigs and start-ups, Waxman has opened the deliciously classic and inventive Washington Park in Manhattan, and New York is happy to have him back.

½ cup white wine
½ medium Vidalia onion
½ bunch of parsley
½ teaspoon sea salt
2 live Maine lobsters, each 1¼ pound
½ bunch of baby arugula
1 pound fava beans
¼ cup good-quality Tuscan extra-virgin olive oil (Tuscan oil
    has more of a peppery bite than other Italian olive oils)
½ teaspoon lemon juice
½ small shallot, peeled and minced
½ small fennel bulb, shaved in fine slivers
Salt and pepper

Make a water bath for the lobsters using wine, onion, parsley, and $\frac{1}{2}$ quart of water. Season with sea salt. Cook for 1 hour; strain. Heat strained bath until boiling, add lobsters, and cook for 7 minutes, until they turn bright red and antennae snap when bent. Remove and let cool.

Clean lobster claws, bodies, and knuckles and set meat aside; place shells in bath, and cook bath at low boil for 1 hour. Remove shells and reduce liquid by half.

Slice lobster tails in half; remove dark vein from tail by using the tip of a knife. Keep tails chilled.

Wash and dry arugula. Shell the fava pods—they will yield approximately $\frac{3}{4}$ cup beans. Heat 1 quart of water to a boil and salt it. Boil beans for 3 minutes. Let cool, then peel off their inner shell.

Make a dressing with the olive oil, lemon juice, and shallot, and add $\frac{1}{4}$ cup lobster cooking juices. Assemble salad by tossing lobster, arugula, dressing, fava beans, and shaved fennel. Season with salt and pepper, and serve at room temperature.

Suggested wine: dry riesling or albariño

Risotto alla Milanese

from Lidia Bastianich, owner, Felidia

"For me sexy food is food that is mellow, that fills one's senses with caressing pleasures and induces a pronounced sense of well-being and a need to share," says Lidia Bastianich. "I think risotto's popularity has to do with the fact that it's the kind of food that embraces you and holds you tight. It comforts the soul." This recipe proves her point. Bastianich remains truthful to the Milanese classic while adding her own special touch.

Proprietor, and co-proprietor with her son Joseph, of several of the country's best Italian restaurants, including the renowned Felidia in New York, Bastianich has her own public television show and a host of culinary awards and has taught courses on the history and anthropology of food. Yet her delight at being at the stove and down-to-earth manner make it clear that for her "the service of a meal is an act of love."

In the case of saffron it is the stigma itself—the actual sex organ of the crocus plant—that is eaten and prized as an aphrodisiac. Just a pinch of richly colored saffron lends a golden hue and subtle flavoring to a number of classic dishes: paella, risotto, bouillabaisse, and cakes. Saffron fulfills a key criterion for a luxury item: It is the most expensive spice in the world.

CHEF'S LOVE MENU

3½ cups hot meat stock kept at a low boil (beef is best, but
    chicken will do)
¼ teaspoon saffron
1½ tablespoons extra-virgin olive oil
½ cup minced onion
1 tablespoon minced shallot
1 cup Arborio or Carnaroli rice
¼ cup dry white wine
¼ teaspoon salt, plus additional if needed
1 ounce beef marrow, cut into ¼-inch pieces (optional; see note)
1 tablespoon unsalted butter, cut into pieces
¼ cup freshly grated Parmesan cheese
Pepper, freshly ground

Pour ½ cup of the hot stock over the saffron in a small heatproof
bowl. Let it steep.

In a heavy, wide 3- to 4-quart casserole or pot, heat the olive oil
over medium heat. Cook the onion and shallot together until
golden, stirring often, about 8 minutes. Add the rice and stir to coat
with the oil until rice edges become translucent, 1 to 2 minutes.

Pour in the wine and stir well until evaporated. Add ½ cup of
the remaining hot stock and ¼ teaspoon salt. Cook, stirring constantly, until all the stock has been absorbed. Stir in the beef marrow, if using. Continue to add hot stock in small batches—just
enough to completely moisten the rice—and cook until each succes-
sive batch has been absorbed.

About 10 minutes after the first addition of stock, stir in the saffron mixture. Stir constantly and adjust the level of heat so the rice is simmering very gently; cook until the rice mixture is creamy but al dente, 6 to 10 minutes.

Remove the casserole from the heat. Beat in the butter until completely melted and then beat in the cheese. Adjust the seasoning with salt, if necessary, and pepper. Serve immediately, ladled into warm shallow bowls.

Note: Few butchers sell beef marrow separately anymore, but it is easy to come up with your own. For about 2 ounces of marrow, start with five or six 1- to 1 1/2-inch beef marrow bones. (Your butcher can supply them and cut them to the correct size.) Heat the stock for the risotto and warm the bones in the stock two at a time for 3 minutes. Remove the bones with a slotted spoon and let them stand just until cool enough to handle. Try to push the marrow through the bone with your finger; it should come right out. If not, use a small spoon to scoop it out. The marrow may be soft around the edges, but the center should still be firm enough to chop.

Suggested wine: rich, not lean, chardonnay

An Italian Folktale

The Duomo in Milano, known for its magnificent Gothic structure with icicle-like steeples, also has beautiful stained-glass windows. The resident glazer at the time, proud of his work in progress, decided to plan his daughter's wedding party within the unfinished Duomo. The preparation of the food was set in his laboratory. Milano is the city of risotto, and, of course, for such a celebration a big pot of risotto was bubbling away for the event. In the flurry of activities, a jar of saffron, which was being used to stain the stained-glass windows, fell from a shelf into the risotto. With hungry guests waiting there was no time to cook another pot of risotto, and so it was that the silky, golden Risotto alla Milanese was born.

—as recalled by Lidia Bastianich

Halibut with Beet Puree and Horseradish Emulsion

from Mark Dommen, chef,
COPIA: The American Center for Wine, Food & the Arts

A veteran of many leading French and American restaurants, Mark Dommen is on the line every day, cooking at COPIA's dramatic open kitchen and keeping an eagle eye on everything and everybody. The appeal of sitting at the counter watching him and his crew cook is matched by the pleasure of this luscious, creamy-textured fish dish. Here's what he says about it: "The seductively smooth, slightly sweet red beet puree works as the perfect back-drop for the delicately poached, pale white fish. Sure to set the tone for the rest of the night to follow."

The puree:
1 tablespoon butter
1 large shallot, chopped into small pieces
1 medium beet or two small beets, peeled and chopped into
    small pieces
Sea salt
Pepper, freshly ground
Vegetable stock to cover, ½ to 1 cup

The emulsion:
2 teaspoons horseradish
1 tablespoon grapeseed oil
¼ teaspoon sea salt, plus additional salt to taste
½ cup vegetable stock
Juice from ½ lemon
⅛ teaspoon pepper, freshly ground
1 tablespoon butter
Pinch cayenne

The fish:
3 baby leeks
1 cup extra-virgin olive oil, plus 1 tablespoon
1 sprig thyme
1 bay leaf
1 sprig savory
2 fillets Alaskan halibut, each 6 ounces; check for pieces of
    bone in fillet and remove with tweezers
Sea salt
Pepper, freshly ground

The garnish:
2 golden beets, roasted at 375 degrees for 45 minutes to
    1 hour
Few small beet tops

Prepare beet puree. Melt ½ tablespoon butter in a small saucepan, add the shallot, and allow to sweat for a couple minutes; then add the beet and sweat for a couple minutes longer. Lightly season with salt and pepper and cover with vegetable stock. Bring the mixture to a boil, then turn down to a low flame and allow to cook until all the vegetable stock has reduced. The shallot and beet should be fully cooked. Transfer to a blender, add the remaining butter, and blend to a fine puree. Taste and add more salt and pepper if necessary. Cover and set aside, keeping warm.

Next prepare the horseradish emulsion. Peel the horseradish and chop into small pieces. Put into a blender, cover with grapeseed oil and half the salt, and blend on high speed until you have a very fine puree. In a small saucepan, combine the vegetable stock with the horseradish puree, lemon juice, and remaining salt and pepper to taste. Bring to a boil. Add the butter and blend, using a hand blender or conventional blender, until the mixture is emulsified. Check the seasoning and balance out the flavor with salt, pepper, lemon juice, and a pinch of cayenne. Set aside and keep warm. You will need to blend it a final time when you are ready to plate the dish.

Move on to the halibut and leeks. Wash the baby leeks very well, making sure to remove all dirt and sand. Blanch them in boiling salted water until tender and then plunge into ice water to stop the cooking. Remove leeks from the ice water and cut them into 1 to 1½-inch pieces.

Put the olive oil in a sauté pan large enough to hold both halibut fillets; add thyme, bay leaf, and savory to oil, and heat to 200 degrees. Season the fish with salt and pepper and put it into the olive oil to poach. You can judge the temperature of the oil by the size of the bubbles coming off the fish. If the oil is too hot, the bubbles will be small and racing to the surface. If the oil is the correct temperature for poaching, the bubbles will be big and rise to the surface very slowly. The fish should take 10 to 12 minutes to cook.

While the fish is cooking, reheat the beet puree and double-check the seasoning. Sauté the leeks in the remaining tablespoon of olive oil in a hot sauté pan for several minutes, letting them caramelize slightly. Briefly reheat the horseradish emulsion in a small sauce pan. When the fish is cooked, transfer it from the pan onto a plate lined with paper towels to absorb any excess olive oil.

To plate, divide the beet puree between two large soup bowls, and spoon the sautéed leeks into the center of the puree. Place the fish on top of the beet puree. Blend the horseradish emulsion and spoon it around the fish. Garnish each fish with a roasted golden beet and some small beet tops. Serve immediately.

Suggested wine: pinot grigio or light pinot noir

Mocha Crème Brûlée

from Maggie Radzwiller, chef and restaurant consultant

"What Maggie Radzwiller doesn't know about the restaurant business isn't worth knowing," says John Mariani in Esquire *magazine. She has opened, consulted at, or redesigned over two dozen restaurants, coast to coast, north to south. Understandably, she has an encyclopedia of recipes at her beck and call. She says that this is her favorite seduction dessert and adds that anything she cooks is sexy, as long as she does it in her chef whites—just the top, that is.*

> 1 cup heavy cream
> ½ vanilla bean, split
> Very small pinch of salt
> 4 tablespoons sugar
> 2 egg yolks
> 1 ounce high-quality chocolate syrup, such as Ghirardelli
> 1 teaspoon instant espresso

Preheat a nonconvection oven to 300 degrees. On the stovetop, heat on medium low the cream, vanilla bean, salt, and 1 tablespoon of the sugar, whisking often. Remove from heat when the mixture reaches 180 degrees. Remove the vanilla bean, scrape the seeds into the pan, and dispose of the pod. Mix another 2 tablespoons of the

CHEF'S LOVE MENU

sugar with the egg yolks in a separate bowl. Whisk the egg yolk mixture very slowly into the cream mixture until the two are completely combined. Add the chocolate syrup and the espresso. Pour this mixture through a fine strainer.

Turn the oven down to 275 degrees.

Place two brûlée dishes in an oven–safe container that isn't much bigger than the dishes. Divide the cream mixture between the dishes. Pour hot water into the container until it is two thirds up to the outside of the brûlée dishes. (You can also pour the water into the container after you have placed it in the oven.)

Bake until barely set, about 30 minutes. The brûlée should wiggle slightly when the container is moved.

Chill for at least 6 hours or preferably overnight.

Sprinkle the remaining tablespoon of sugar on brûlées and shake the dishes to distribute the sugar evenly across the top (don't use a utensil such as a spoon to spread the sugar). Caramelize the sugar by putting the brûlée dishes under the broiler for a minute or two, or use one of those newfangled home kitchen torches: Hold the torch at an angle and just touch the sugar with the flame until it browns. Allow the sugar to "crust" for about 2 minutes before eating.

3

{xotic {venings

★ Moroccan Love Dishs ★
★ Cumin Carrots ★
★ Couscous and Chickpeas with
Red Pepper and Lemon Zest ★
★ Moroccan Chicken with Olives
and Preserved Lemons ★
★ Date Delight ★
★ Candied Rose Petals ★

he *Kama Sutra* was translated into English by Richard Burton in 1883 with instructions to men to "do to a woman what he likes best" or to employ ointments to "subjugate a woman's will." For generations this version was considered the definitive erotic text. Now a new translation affirms that Burton egregiously underplayed passages addressing women's sexual pleasure and the role of women in erotic love play. The translators of the new edition maintain that "the *Kama Sutra* is about pleasure in a much broader sense—good food and good drink, wearing beautiful silk clothing, going on picnics, listening to good music." And women definitely don't play a secondhand role. After all, in the classic Tantric tradition, the man assumes the lotus position and is straddled by the woman. So don't sit idly in the harem waiting for your sheikh: Go forth, *Kama Sutra* in hand, and take the leading role in seduction.

Set the stage: Fill your kitchen with fragrances of cardamom and cloves, cinnamon and vanilla, a dizzying mix of spices to perfume your Arabian nights. Crank up the Ravi Shankar, pop in a *Casablanca* video, and heat up the essential oils that are key to any aromatic aphrodisiac repertory—sensual sandalwood, cedar, and ylang ylang. Create subtle lighting with fragrant candles or rose-colored silk draped over a lamp. Eat on the floor on silk cushions. Cover your bed with vibrant red and yellow silks, and lead your lover to it with a trail of candied rose petals.

Take a cue from the Arabs, who, in their customs and books of old, were highly attentive to creating seductive environments that appealed to all the senses. Read the instructions of another ancient book, the twelfth-century *Ananga Ranga*, an impeccable guide to creating atmosphere, to your love:

> . . . *place musical instruments, especially the pipe and the lute; refreshments, as cocoa-nut, betel-leaf and milk, which is useful for retaining*

*and restoring vigor . . . and books gladdening the glance with illustra-
tions of love-postures and containing amorous songs.*

    Splendid divalgiri, *or wall lights, should gleam all around the
hall, reflected by a hundred mirrors, whilst both man and woman
should contend against any reserve, or false shame, giving themselves
up in complete nakedness to unrestrained voluptuousness, upon a high
and handsome bedstead, raised on tall legs and furnished with many
pillows, and covered by a rich* chatra *or canopy; the sheets being be-
sprinkled with flowers and the coverlet scented by burning luscious
incense, such as aloes and other fragrant woods.*

Has anyone come up with a better description of how to ignite an
evening and excite a lover?

Moroccan Love Disks

This dish was something I had in Tunisia one early May after a trip to Pantelleria—an Italian island but one closer to Tunisia than Sicily—proved to be a disaster. The sirocco winds circled the house relentlessly, howling like mad, making the whole experience like an endless Wuthering Heights.

But Tunisia, 40 kilometers across the Mediterranean, could nearly be glimpsed and was only a ferry ride away. This dish, more Moroccan than Tunisian, is a variation of the first thing I ate in Tunisia. What made it provocative were the soft slippery inside of the eggplant, the crisp exterior, the cinnamon that lent it an exotic fragrance, and the turquoise-eyed young man who followed me everywhere that first day . . .

2 tablespoons flour
Salt and pepper to taste
½ tablespoons confectioners' sugar
½ teaspoon cumin
½ teaspoon nutmeg
½ teaspoon cinnamon
½ cup vegetable oil
1 medium-size Japanese eggplant, peeled and cut into
    ½-inch round slices
1 teaspoon chopped fresh mint

Mix the flour with salt and pepper on a medium-size plate. In a bowl, mix the sugar with the cumin, nutmeg, and cinnamon, and set aside.

Heat the oil in a medium-size frying pan while you dredge the eggplant in the flour. When the oil is smoking hot, add the eggplant slices, one by one, and cook until they are golden brown, about 1 minute. Have tongs ready so that when they start to brown—it happens quickly—you can flip them over. Cook the rounds through on the other side, about 30 seconds, remove, and drain on paper towels.

Arrange the eggplant on a dish, and sprinkle with the sugar-spice mixture and then the mint. Serve hot.

> *A robust constitution is indispensable for copulation, but, above all, play with her lovingly, until she is excited and full of desire.*
>
> —Vatsayana, *Kama Sutra*

Cumin Carrots

We know they're nutritious, and if you follow the ancients' line of thinking, the shape of this vegetable is certainly suggestive. Yes, carrots were considered an aphrodisiac by Greeks and Arabs, and for good reason: Vitamin A doesn't just enhance eyesight; it's also a key component in the production of sex hormones and stimulation of the libido for both sexes.

When I was 21, Saleh Salim, the revered Egyptian soccer star who had put his country on the world sports map, took me through the Cairo souk. I saw more varieties of eggplants, melons, and vibrant spices in sacks that day than I had ever imagined existed. Later, I became friendly with a family that traced its lineage back to the Phoenicians. Meals in their house were redolent of exotic spices, consumed as the Nile cast lazy blue and purple reflections across their high, water-stained ceiling.

I did not bed the older Englishman who was courting me at the time, but I left Egypt with a genie's lamp full of recipes that were well used in subsequent amorous adventures.

1 tablespoon butter
1 teaspoon finely chopped fresh ginger
½ teaspoon mustard seeds
4 or 5 carrots, each scrubbed well, quartered lengthwise,
    then cut crosswise into 4 pieces
¼ cup dry white wine
¼ teaspoon cumin

Salt and pepper
1 tablespoon fresh lemon juice
½ orange, peeled, seeded, and chopped into 1½-inch
   pieces
⅛ cup chopped pistachios
2 tablespoons fresh parsley
2 tablespoons fresh cilantro

Melt butter in medium–size frying pan. Add ginger and mustard seeds, and sauté for 2 to 3 minutes. Add carrots and sauté for 2 to 3 minutes, turning occasionally, until the pan is dry. Add wine. Cover and cook until carrots are tender, about 5 minutes. Add the cumin and salt and pepper to taste, and cook uncovered until wine evaporates. If carrots dry out, add a small amount of water.

    Transfer to a bowl, add lemon juice, orange pieces, pistachios, parsley, and cilantro and toss. Cool to room temperature.

Couscous and Chickpeas with Red Pepper and Lemon Zest

Couscous and chickpeas are a perfect marriage of starch and protein and have a delightful combination of toothsome texture and flavor. This is one of my favorite side dishes, and it livens up a wide variety of fish, chicken, and meat dishes.

1 red pepper
2 tablespoons olive oil
4 ounces chickpeas, cooked (or canned) and drained
1 tablespoon butter
Few threads of saffron
½ teaspoon salt plus additional for dressing
1 cup water
1 cup precooked package of couscous (Tipiak, a French
    brand, is preferable)
Juice and zest from half a lemon
1 teaspoon chopped mint
½ teaspoon fennel powder (available at specialty stores) or
    ¼ cup fresh fennel tops, chopped
Pepper
¼ cup chopped parsley

Preheat broiler. Place bell pepper on baking sheet and roast under the broiler, turning once each side is charred, until blackened all over. Remove from oven and let sit until cool, then peel, cut off both ends, seed, and remove membranes. Cut pepper into strips.

Heat a medium-size skillet. Add 1 tablespoon of the olive oil and when it is hot, add only enough of the chickpeas to make one layer in the pan. Cook over medium heat, shaking the pan to coat, until chickpeas are lightly browned and slightly crisp, 3 to 4 minutes. Repeat with remaining chickpeas.

In a medium-size saucepan, combine butter, saffron, $1/2$ teaspoon salt and water, and bring to a boil. Add couscous, stir thoroughly, and cover. Let sit for 5 minutes.

Whisk remaining tablespoon of oil into lemon juice until blended. Add lemon zest, mint, and fennel powder. Add salt and pepper to taste.

Fluff couscous well with fork and transfer to serving bowl. Add red pepper strips, toasted chickpeas, and parsley, combine with dressing, and serve.

Moroccan Chicken with Olives and Preserved Lemons

Adapted from Paula Wolfert,
Couscous and Other Good Food from Morocco

Noted food critic Gael Greene has called Paula Wolfert "a sensualist . . . a highwire kitchen improvisationist." Certainly she is someone engaged in a long-standing love affair with the world of Mediterranean food.

Wolfert said, "My life seems to revolve around finding new recipes— food with plenty of flavor that lingers in the mouth. Such food appeals to all my senses; every nuance has a meaning. To me, good food is memory. One time or another, I've had a fling with each of the recipes in my books."

This is a dish that is recognized for its international appeal. Zarela Martinez, chef and owner of New York's top Mexican restaurant, Zarela, said, "I love a chicken tagine with preserved lemons and green olives, and slightly sweet eggplant on the side with a pomegranate-molasses vinaigrette. . . . Whenever I'm trying to seduce someone, let's say, that's exactly the meal that I'll make."

> 1 medium-size chicken, cut into 6 pieces, with liver set aside
> 3 cloves garlic, chopped
> 1 to 2 tablespoons salt
> ¼ teaspoon saffron, crushed
> ¼ teaspoon turmeric

½ cup grated onion, drained
¼ cup olive oil
1 teaspoon fresh ginger
¼ teaspoon cumin
¼ teaspoon cayenne
¼ teaspoon paprika
¼ cup chopped fresh parsley
¼ cup chopped fresh cilantro
2 cups water
½ cup green olives, pitted (look for Greek or Italian brands that
    are somewhat bitter, often called green "cracked" olives)
Juice of 1 lemon
¼ preserved lemon (see page 70)

Wash chicken pieces in salted water, drain, and rub with a mixture of two-thirds of the garlic and the salt. Rinse again.

Mix saffron with turmeric. Place onions, chicken, olive oil, remaining garlic, ginger, cumin, saffron–turmeric mixture, cayenne, paprika, parsley, and cilantro in a pot. Cover with 2 cups water and bring to a boil, then reduce heat to medium and simmer for 30 minutes, turning the chicken often in the sauce.

Add olives, lemon juice, and preserved lemon to pot and cook 10 minutes, uncovered. Mash liver against side of pan to incorporate into sauce. Transfer chicken to ovenproof platter and discard neck and back. Brown in oven while reducing sauce another 10 minutes or until sauce reaches soupy consistency.

Suggested wine: pinot grigio

Date Delight

Dates are said to be the oldest cultivated plant on the planet, and they figure prominently in the Bible and in Middle Eastern and Mediterranean cuisines. The Medjhool date is one of the largest and best. In California or in specialty gourmet stores fresh dates on the stem can be found when in season, fall through spring, and they are a delightful treat.

These dates can be poached up to a day in advance. But if you don't have time or if your love is nibbling on your neck, a simple alternative is just to skip to the end of the recipe: split the dates lengthwise, remove their seeds, stuff each with about a teaspoon of mascarpone or blue cheese and a walnut, and devour.

½ bottle light red wine, such as Beaujolais or Italian Merlot
Juice and zest of half an orange
1 vanilla bean, split
1 cinnamon stick or ½ teaspoon ground cinnamon
4 Medjhool dates
⅛ cup honey
½ tablespoon peppercorns
4 teaspoons mascarpone cheese or blue cheese
4 walnuts, whole pieces

EXOTIC EVENINGS

Bring wine, orange juice, vanilla bean, and cinnamon to a slow boil in a small saucepan, and lower heat to a simmer. Add dates and poach until their skins start to pucker. Remove dates from pan with a slotted spoon, slip off the skins, then slit the dates lengthwise and remove seeds.

Add the honey, peppercorns, and orange zest to the wine mixture and simmer until the liquid is reduced to half, 15 to 20 minutes. Strain liquid.

Place 1 teaspoon mascarpone and a walnut in each date. Pool sauce on two small serving plates and place dates in center.

The prepared dates can be kept in the refrigerator for 3 to 4 days.

Candied Rose Petals

Rose petals were liberally sprinkled about during medieval feasts, where many of the participants frolicked about nude and generally behaved as decadently as the Romans did during their orgies. Sprinkle these petals to make a trail to your lair . . .

> 1 egg white
> 1 teaspoon water
> Sugar
> 50 rose petals, just picked

Beat the egg white with water in a small bowl until it is frothy and broken down.

Place the rose petals one at a time in a small strainer and dip into the egg mixture to thinly coat, then sprinkle sugar on each side of each petal. Sprinkle a large plate or dinner plate with sugar and place the petals on it. Let dry for at least an hour.

Note: Violets and fruit tree blossoms such as plum or citrus are also good candying candidates.

O Love what hours were thine and mine,
In lands of palm and southern pine;
In lands of palm, of orange-blossom,
Of olive, aloe, and maize and vine.

—Alfred, Lord Tennyson

Fruit Cocktail
Pomegranate Loving Cup

The pomegranate as long had a symbolic association wither fertility in many cultures. No wonder; the fruit itself is visually seductive—round and taut, spilling forth sparkling, wet-looking, bright red seeds.

4 pomegranates
½ cup rosé or light-bodied red wine
¼ to ⅓ cup honey, to taste depending on sweet-
    ness of fruit
1 whole clove or ⅛ teaspoon ground clove
Scant ⅛ teaspoon ground nutmeg
Scant ⅛ teaspoon ground ginger
½ teaspoon ground cinnamon
¼ blood orange or orange

Place, wine, honey, and spices in medium–size enamel saucepan, then simmer for 5 minutes. Remove clove if using. Grate orange peel into the mixture, then squeeze in juice from the orange.

Peel skin off two of the pomegranates. Cut all four pomegranates in half horizontally, and scoop out seeds and pits. Reserve two of the pomegranates as "cups" and their seeds for use later. Squeeze seeds of two of the pomegranates, and use a strainer to extract maximum juice.

Add the pomegranate juice to other mixture. Pour drink into "cups," add seeds, and serve.

4

Seafood Bacchanalia

★ Oysters with Ponzu Sauce ★
★ Citrus-Cured Salmon with Green Apple
and Tomato-Tarragon Emulsion ★
★ Mushroom Soup with Scallops ★
★ Grilled Swordfish with Orange
and Oregano Salsa ★
★ Raspberry Soufflé ★

It seems there are two camps as to what constitutes the most seductive love feast, one holding that decadence is the order of the day—
indulging in foie gras, chocolate, and other rich, fatty foods—and
the other proclaiming that lust and love are best served by amorous
offerings that are light yet stimulating. As that applies to fish, the
fattier varieties such as salmon, particularly smoked salmon and

smoked fish of any sort, along with tuna, sardines, and anchovies, are often touted as the most stimulating to desire. But the lighter-colored and lighter-fleshed fish can be just as persuasive.

Whatever your preference, there's a philosophy to support it. Fish and all sorts of shellfish have been idolized for eons, most notably by Egyptians, Romans, and Greeks. Many ancient cultures have documented the significant place fish holds in their culture—think of Etruscan frescoes—symbolizing life itself. And, of course, there are few societies that don't tout some form of seafood as a sexual vitalizer. Start to bait your mate with the hallowed oyster, incubator of Aphrodite, the goddess of love.

You are a garden locked up,
my sister, my bride . . .
Your plants are an orchard of
pomegranates with choice fruits.

—Song of Songs 4:12–13

Oysters with Ponzu Sauce

What other food raises the aphrodisiac antennae more profoundly? When oysters, like champagne, enter the scene, the sexual radar of everyone in the room perks up. Where to start with the list of the oyster's attributes?

The Romans prized the mollusk for its use in orgies, and emperors reputedly paid for oysters by their weight in gold. Casanova was said to eat 50 oysters a day; passing them from his mouth into a young lover's was part of his seduction ritual. The oyster occupies a relevant position in still-life paintings of the seventeenth century, at times alluding to a patron's social standing and at other times symbolizing an aphrodisiac. Perhaps Aphrodite springing from the pearl was a reference to a pearl nestled in the oyster's two halves, a paean to female physiology and sexuality.

Medical research substantiates the oyster's prowess. High levels of zinc cause it to activate a key enzyme in testosterone production. The oyster also acts on the glands that stimulate both men's and women's sexual desire, glands that produce natural lubricants.

Creaminess; a clean, briny, sweet aroma; and a clear liquid when opened are all signs that the oyster is ready to be enjoyed.

2 tablespoons mirin
5 tablespoons soy sauce
1 tablespoon thinly sliced scallion
½ cup rice wine vinegar
2 tablespoons lemon juice
2 tablespoons lime juice
12 of your favorite oysters, washed and drained (see note)
1 ounce caviar or sea urchin roe (optional)

Prepare ponzu sauce ahead of time.

To prepare sauce: In a small saucepan, bring mirin, soy sauce, scallion, vinegar, lemon juice, and lime juice to a full boil, then immediately turn off the heat and chill the sauce.

Pry open oysters over the sink, using an oyster knife. Loosen the oyster but leave it in half the shell. Arrange crushed ice on serving platter and place oysters in shells on ice. When ponzu sauce is cold, pour it over the oysters and serve. Top with caviar, if desired.

Note: In northern California I prefer local Kumomotos, a small, sweet, and succulent variety native to Japan that is now grown in Pacific coastal waters. Also, if you are not comfortable wielding an oyster knife, you can buy shucked oysters as long as the oysters have been shucked within 3 hours of the time you will be serving them. Have the fishmonger reserve the shells for you.

Citrus-Cured Salmon with Green Apple and Tomato-Tarragon Emulsion

My friend Marty, a personal chef and wine expert, tells this story: "To me the most romantic dinners are prepared outside my own kitchen and entail a surprise. My girlfriend and I were staying at a guesthouse in the Napa Valley. She thought we were going out to dinner, but here we were, nestled in a beautiful little piece of paradise, so I decided to prepare an intimate, unexpected dinner in the tiny kitchen. I wanted something fresh and light with clean, vivid flavors that I could prep ahead. This dish, followed by a ripe goat Brie and some red grapes, set the 'love menu' for our weekend."

The fish:
3 tablespoons kosher salt
2 tablespoons sugar
Zest of 1 lemon
Zest of 1 orange
1 teaspoon Dijon mustard
1 bunch of tarragon, minced
1 center-cut salmon fillet, about 1 pound

The sauce:
1 teaspoon soy sauce
1 teaspoon mirin

The emulsion:
2 large ripe tomatoes, cored and coarsely chopped
¾ teaspoon salt
2 sprigs tarragon, coarsely chopped
½ teaspoon extra-virgin olive oil
Squeeze of lemon juice

The garnishes:
½ Granny Smith apple
Few squeezes of lemon juice
¼ teaspoon wasabi (optional)
4 or 5 tarragon leaves
2 tablespoons peeled, seeded, and diced tomato

To prepare the citrus cure for the fish, combine the salt, sugar, lemon and orange zests, mustard, and tarragon in a bowl and mix well.

Remove pin bones from the salmon fillet with tweezers (or ask your fishmonger to do this for you). Place salmon fillet skin side down on plastic wrap and spread the citrus cure over meat side, covering completely. Wrap fish tightly in the plastic and place on a small pan. Place another pan on top of fish and weight with a small sauté pan or other object. Be careful not to use something too heavy, as it will damage the fish. Place in the refrigerator for 24 hours.

Remove salmon from plastic wrap and completely rinse off the citrus cure mixture.

For the sauce, combine soy sauce and mirin in a small container and reserve.

Begin preparing the emulsion by putting tomatoes and salt in a blender and pureeing thoroughly. Place a double thickness of cheesecloth in a fine mesh strainer set over a bowl. Gently pour the tomato puree into the strainer. Let sit for 4 hours or overnight in the refrigerator. When you remove the bowl from the refrigerator there should be about $^2/_3$ cup completely clear tomato "water" in the bowl. Stir the tarragon into the tomato water. Refrigerate in a covered container for 1 to 2 hours.

For the apple garnish, peel the apple and finely grate it into a small bowl. Add lemon juice and mix well. Cover and reserve.

To complete the tomato emulsion, strain the tarragon out of tomato water, then place tomato water, olive oil, and lemon juice in a blender and puree until frothy.

To serve the dish, remove the skin from the salmon fillet and cut, on the bias, two $3^1/_4$-inch–thick slices per person. (You can also remove each slice from the skin as you cut it.)

Fan salmon slices in the center of a rimmed soup bowl. Pour a few drops of soy–mirin sauce over salmon, then about $^1/_4$ cup tomato emulsion around it. Place a dollop of grated apple on each salmon slice, then top with wasabi (if using) and tarragon leaves. Sprinkle diced tomatoes around plate and serve.

SEAFOOD BACCHANALIA

Note: *The dish can be plated without the tomato emulsion and held at room temperature for up to 10 minutes. This short hold time will allow you to enjoy a glass of wine and arrive at the table in a totally relaxed fashion. In this case, froth the tomato emulsion and add it to the plate at the last minute.*

Suggested wine: riesling

> *I don't know whether you've ever had a woman eat an apple while you were doing it. . . . You can imagine how that affects you.*
>
> —Henry Miller, *Tropic of Capricorn*

Mushroom Soup with Scallops

Perhaps it has something to do with the way they suddenly sprout out of the earth, and the fact that they are lethal if you don't know how to identify or handle them—mushrooms are sexy. Certainly their earthy fragrance and meaty texture make the life of many a vegetarian, as well as the lives of many lovers, more satisfing.

Combining a velvety mushroom soup with silky scallops creates an enticing and delectable dish—and perhaps that's all you will need, or want, for dinner. The addition of truffle oil gives the soup an erotic spike.

½ pound shiitake mushrooms
½ pound Portabello mushroom caps
¼ cup lightly salted butter
1 tablespoon finely minced shallot
4 tablespoons Madeira
2 tablespoons white truffle oil
2 cups mushroom broth (available at specialty grocery stores)
1 cup heavy cream
Salt and pepper
2 "diver" or top-quality sea scallops
1 tablespoon chopped parsley

Cut ¼ inch off the bottoms of the shiitake mushrooms. Clean both the shiitake and Portabello mushrooms if gritty. Cut the mushrooms into ¼-inch slices.

Heat a sauté pan on a medium flame and then add the butter. As soon as the butter is completely melted, add the sliced mushrooms and the shallot. Cook them until they are completely tender. Turn up the heat and then add the Madeira. Remove the pan from the heat. Drizzle the white truffle oil on the mixture.

Put the mushroom mixture into a blender or food processor fitted with a steel blade. Puree. Slowly add the mushroom broth and heavy cream until all the ingredients are smooth. Pour the soup into a small saucepan and bring to a simmer. Add salt and pepper to taste.

Put the sauté pan back on the flame. Bring the heat up to high. Place the scallops in the pan and cook for about 1 minute on each side. Remove the pan from the heat.

Pour soup into wide-rim soup bowls or shallow pasta bowls. Place a scallop in the center of each bowl and garnish with parsley.

Suggested wine: chardonnay

Grilled Swordfish with Orange and Oregano Salsa

Certainly the swordfish is a symbolic sort of fish, a kind of unicorn of the deep, and quite a spectacular sight plunging into the ocean, its swordlike prow aloft. It has a flavor that distinguishes it from most other white-fleshed fish and a firm texture that allows you to handle it as you would tuna. I would not have thought of using oregano with swordfish, but I learned this from an Italian Calabrese, who, of course, learned it from his mama. I have never known an Italian man who did not possess at least one good mama's recipe.

One summer I shared a house in the Hamptons with this Calabrese and a posse of Italians. One disadvantage of such a situation is that you get hustled into the back of an Alpha Spider at one o'clock in the morning (after you've already been out for the night) and whisked away to parties with people wearing togas and drinking Pimms. The advantage is that you learn how to cook at least one good Italian dish, and there will be plenty of flirting and laughing in the process. On the Fourth of July that summer, I switched nationalities: I invited a German to our house for dinner and spent the evening with him, hidden in the dunes in his pink Cadillac convertible, watching—and creating—fireworks.

2 tablespoons chopped fresh oregano
1½ cups peeled, cored, and diced orange pieces
Juice of 2 lemons
1 teaspoon finely diced serrano chile
2 swordfish steaks, each 7 ounces and about ¾ inch thick
1 tablespoon extra-virgin olive oil
Salt and pepper

Combine oregano, diced orange, lemon juice, and serrano chile and let sit for at least 1 hour.

Baste swordfish with olive oil, salt, and pepper. Grill fish for 3 minutes on each side at a high heat.

Plate fish, pour salsa over the top, and serve.

Suggested wine: savennières or vouvray

Raspberry Soufflé

Jacqueline Margulin has been running Cafe Jacqueline, the romantic little restaurant in San Francisco's North Beach that serves only soufflés every evening, for 22 years. You can order soup or salad to start, but the only other menu choices involve what kind of ethereal soufflé you prefer—Gruyère, leek, or lobster? White corn, ginger, or garlic?

"Chocolate is perhaps the most romantic," she says, although raspberry is a close runner-up. "All soufflés are romantic," Margulin says; the couples in her café feed each other the soufflé. Her Valentine's Day reservations pour in a year in advance from romantics such as the gentleman who put the ring inside the rose inside the soufflé. This Bordeaux native says she never tires of concocting the most romantic of dishes for her customers. "I see everything," she says with a smile and Gallic savoir faire. "I am in the kitchen, baking the soufflé, but I am also watching the romance."

Ultimately, it's their transformative powers that put food and love on the same scale. The radical alchemy of a humble egg transformed into a soufflé is like the moment when titillation ignites into sexual love and our lives are changed. The potency is irrefutable. This recipe, a variation of Jacqueline's, is a recognition of that equation.

Butter for greasing soufflé dishes
¼ cup granulated sugar plus scant additional for dusting
    soufflé dishes
1 egg, separated

1 tablespoon unsalted butter, cold
Pinch of salt
2 tablespoons flour
¼ cup half-and-half
½ teaspoon cream of tartar
¼ cup raspberries, washed, dried, and halved, but not broken
Confectioners' sugar

Preheat oven to 400 degrees. Butter two 10-ounce soufflé dishes and coat with granulated sugar, shaking out excess. Using electric mixer at high speed, beat 2 tablespoons of the granulated sugar, the egg yolk, butter, and salt in a large bowl until thoroughly mixed. Sift flour over mixture and fold in.

Scald half-and-half (bring it just to the boiling point), then add egg yolk mixture. Set aside. Whisk egg white with cream of tartar until soft peaks form; then gradually add remaining 2 tablespoons granulated sugar and whisk by hand or with an electric mixer at high speed until whites form stiff peaks. Quickly fold the egg white into the egg yolk mixture, then, before the ingredients are completely incorporated, add the raspberries. Blend thoroughly but don't overmix.

Divide batter between soufflé dishes, filling to within half an inch of the top and put the soufflé dishes on a baking sheet. Bake 10 to 12 minutes or until puffed and golden and a little wobbly in the center. Sprinkle with confectioners' sugar and serve immediately.

Culinary Quickie

Citrus

In many cultures, particularly Mediterranean ones, meat and fish dishes are served with just a squeeze or a wedge of lemon or orange, fruits that transform and highlight a dish with their juice, fragrance, and flavor. I squeeze lemon into just about everything—soups, fruit salads, lentils, pasta dishes, stews (of both Eastern and Western origin)—and I use lemon and orange zest liberally. (To capture more of the zest's essential oils, zest directly into a bowl or pot, or place parchment paper underneath, then scrape zest into your container.)

The Greeks and Moroccans sometimes use orange juice and zest where we would think of adding lemon, such as in fish soups. Try some orange instead of lemon juice in your salad dressing.

There are so many kinds of lemons and oranges to choose from—too many to begin to describe here. Suffice it to say that many people find Italy's southern lemons, those from the western Amalfi coast and Sicily, the best—thin skinned and sweet, much like Meyer lemons, now widely grown and available in the United States. Whatever your choice, look for unwaxed lemons, particularly for zesting, and let your imagination tell you when a dab'll do ya. Recall that, as is the case with many fruits and vegetables, the most visually perfect ones do not necessarily have the best taste or character.

Preserved lemons offer a unique taste, salty and intense. There are certain dishes that are just not authentic without them. Preserving lemons is a pleasure: stuffing the fruit with salt and shaking the jar as the lemons turn soft and silken in your refrigerator. Normally it takes a few weeks, although I have come across several methods that hasten the process. The doyenne of Moroccan cooking, Paula Wolfert, insists that there is no replacement for the real thing, although in her book *Couscous and Other Good Food from Morocco*, she does offer a five–day time–saver recipe (although not the one listed here) as well as a traditional thirty–day recipe.

I have included here a recipe that takes a week, one that takes five days, and an ultra–quick lemon sauce for desserts only; it gives something of the taste of preserved lemons without their complexity.

The important thing to observe when preserving lemons is that they must be covered with the salted lemon juice. To use preserved lemons, rinse the portion of the lemon you will use at one time, discard the pulp (if desired), and slice the lemon peel as directed in the recipe you're following. The pickling juice can be reused two or three times, but it should be discarded within the year.

Preserved Lemons

10 large, thin skinned lemons
½ cup coarse or kosher salt, more if necessary

Wash 4 lemons. Quarter them, leaving the stem end intact. Pack salt into the fruit's cavity, reshape the fruit, and place lemons in a 1–quart jar, pushing them down to release their juices and adding more salt after putting each lemon into the jar. Add enough lemon juice to cover (juice from about 6 lemons) and seal tightly, leaving some air space before closing the jar.

Let lemons macerate in a cool, dark place for 1 week, then refrigerate. Preserved lemons will keep, refrigerated, for 6 months to 1 year.

Preserved Lemons, Five-Day Method

6 lemons
¼ cup kosher salt

Squeeze and strain the juice from 4 of the lemons into a pint jar with a glass lid. Thinly slice the remaining 2 lemons, remove any seeds, and add the lemon slices to the jar. Pour the salt over the lemons, close the jar, and shake vigorously.

For the next 5 days, shake the jar vigorously at least once each day.

Quick Lemon Sauce for Desserts

2 lemons
1 cup sugar

Wash lemons. Cut into $1/8$-inch-thick slices. Remove any seeds. In a saucepan, combine the sugar with 1 cup water and stir over moderate heat until sugar is dissolved. Add the lemon slices and simmer over low heat until the syrup becomes thick, about 20 minutes. Let cool to room temperature.

Set aside 12 of the best lemon slices; finely chop the rest. Combine the syrup with the chopped lemon and drizzle over cakes or fruit, and then decorate the dessert with the reserved lemon slices.

This sauce should be used within 1 day.

Fruit Cocktail
Limoncello

Although various versions of it have been enjoyed for years, Limoncello is suddenly the rage in Italy. This drink packs a wallop, so although this may seem like a small quantity, it will last if you enjoy it slowly.

Zest of 2 lemons
⅓ bottle (750 ml.) of vodka, good quality
½ cup sugar

Place zest in a glass 1–quart jar and add the vodka. Cover and seal the jar tightly, then let it sit in a cool spot for approximately 10 to 12 days, or until the zest has colored the vodka deep yellow.

Strain the vodka into a container; reserve the zest.

Combine sugar with 1 cup water in a saucepan and bring to a boil, stirring until the sugar dissolves, then boil the mixture for about 2 to 3 minutes. Pour the boiling liquid over the zest into a container. Let the syrup mixture cool, then discard the zest.

Add the syrup to the vodka and pour into bottles with tight-fitting lids. Let the bottles sit for 5 days. Store in the freezer. Serve chilled.

5

Mediterranean Nights

★ Tempura Squash Blossoms ★
★ Peel-a-Tomato Soup ★
★ Beet, Goat Cheese, and Walnut Salad ★
★ Lamb and Lobster ★
★ Sicilian Cornmeal Cake with
Ruby Red Sauce ★
★ Almond Love Bites ★

*I*taly, Spain, southern France, Greece, and Turkey are all places where indolence isn't highly underrated, as it often seems to be in America. The cuisines of these cultures are rich in sun-kissed fruit and simple, robust, red-blood-in-the-beast flavors. Dining on such foods offers a perfect way to celebrate a romance and travel somewhere in the imagination.

If it's Italy that inspires you, make your own night at the opera at home. You don't need a gondola rocking to recreate Venice. . . .

Tempura Squash Blossoms

The squash flower is a beautiful and fragile thing: its bright canary blossoms are in season for only a very short time. Although squash grows in many climates, its blossoms are mainly used in Mexican, Italian, and Spanish cooking, often fiery cuisines where delicate dishes also thrive. Few things, outside of your lover, are as exciting in your mouth as fried squash blossoms: salty and crunchy outside yielding to a melting creaminess inside.

Preparing squash blossoms may sound difficult but is actually quite easy. Some chefs such as Giuliano Bugialli caution the cook to always remove the pistil from the flower before using, while others say the flowers are fine non castrati. *With the pistil or without doesn't seem to change the taste much. Be careful when stuffing the flowers, because they tear easily.*

Fillings should be juicy, melting, and as imaginative as you like—mozzarella, goat cheese, Mexican fresh cheese, are all commonly used. I like the salty kick of anchovies nestled in the flower's core. The fried blossoms can be served with a fresh tomato and basil sauce or with a mint or pesto sauce.

½ cup flour
1 scant teaspoon olive oil
Soda water or sparkling water
1 egg white
½ teaspoon sea salt
Peanut or vegetable oil for frying

6 to 8 zucchini flowers, thorns removed from base and pistil
   from center
3 to 4 ounces fresh goat cheese or mozzarella
2 tablespoons finely chopped anchovies

Make the batter by sifting flour into a bowl and making a well in the center. Stir in the olive oil, salt, and enough soda water to make a batter the consistency of thick cream. Let stand for 1 hour.

Just before frying, beat egg white into stiff peaks and fold into batter.

Heat the oil in a deep fryer or frying pan until very hot.

Loosely stuff the flowers with about $\frac{1}{2}$ ounce goat cheese and anchovies. A small–size pastry bag attachment does the best job, or you can use a small teaspoon. Twist the tips of the petals to seal. Dip flowers in the batter to coat and then place in the hot oil. Deep fry at 340 degrees until flowers are light brown, 1 to 2 minutes on each side. Drain on paper towels and serve, with sauce if desired, while still hot.

Peel-a-Tomato Soup

from Philippe Jeanty, chef–owner, Bistro Jeanty and Jeanty at Jack's

The name I chose for this soup is not what it's called by Philippe Jeanty, whose restaurants are in Yountville and San Francisco, California, but to me, his luscious, velvety en croûte *soup is definitely come hither. After all, to eat this soup you pierce the crust and then peel it back with your spoon (or is that your tongue?).*

¼ cup plus 1 scant teaspoon unsalted butter
¼ pound yellow onions, sliced
1¼ pounds ripe tomatoes, cored and quartered
3 cloves garlic, peeled
⅛ cup tomato paste
1 small bay leaf
1 scant teaspoon black peppercorns
½ teaspoon fresh thyme leaves
Up to ½ cup water if tomatoes are not juicy (optional)
2 cups heavy cream
Salt
¼ teaspoon freshly ground white pepper
½ pound puff pastry (defrost if frozen)
1 egg white beaten with 1 tablespoon water

Melt the ¼ cup butter in a large stockpot over medium–low heat. Add the onions, cover, and cook for about 5 minutes. Cook until onions are soft and transparent, but do not let them brown. Add tomatoes, garlic, tomato paste, bay leaf, peppercorns, thyme, and—if mixture has too much of a tomato–paste consistency—the water. Simmer over low heat 35 to 40 minutes, until tomatoes and onions are very soft. Puree, either in a blender or using a handheld immersion blender, and then strain through a medium–size strainer. Return the soup to the pot. Add the cream, salt, white pepper, and the remaining butter, to taste.

Let the soup cool for at least 2 hours.

Pour the cooled soup into two soup bowls. Roll out the puff pastry to ¼ inch thick. Cut 2 rounds slightly larger than the bowls. Paint the dough with the egg wash and turn the circles egg–wash side down over the tops of the bowls, pulling lightly on the sides, but taking care not to tear the pastry, to make the dough drum–tight over the top.

Lightly paint the top of the dough rounds with egg wash but don't indent the dough. Bake for 10 to 15 minutes, until the tops are golden brown. As with a soufflé, do not open the oven door for at least 5 minutes, or the tops may collapse. Serve.

Suggested wine: beaujolais or chenin

Beet, Goat Cheese, and Walnut Salad

As far back as Pliny (A.D. 23–79), beets were acknowledged as "guaranteed to inflame the passions."

¼ cup shelled and halved walnuts
1 pound beets (5 or 6 medium or small beets), washed and
   trimmed but not peeled
1 blood orange or regular orange
1 small shallot, finely chopped
⅛ cup balsamic vinegar
¼ cup olive oil
Salt and freshly ground pepper
1 bunch arugula, washed and dried
¼ pound fresh goat cheese
Lemon zest

Preheat oven to 325 degrees. Place nuts on a baking sheet and toast until fragrant and lightly browned, 5 to 8 minutes. Set aside.

Increase the oven heat to 375 degrees. Place the beets in a baking dish, add water to about halfway up the beets, and cover tightly with aluminum foil. Bake for 45 minutes to 1 hour, or until the beets are tender and can be pierced with a fork. Remove from the oven, take off the foil, and when beets are cooled, rub or peel off skins, then cut into small chunks.

MEDITERRANEAN NIGHTS

Zest the orange. Cut the orange in half and squeeze the juice from one of the halves into the zest. Remove the skin and pith from the other half and cut it into small pieces. Peel and dice the shallot and stir into the orange juice and zest. Whisk in the vinegar, oil, salt, and pepper, and set aside.

Place a handful of arugula on each plate. Divide the beets between the two plates. Add a spoonful of goat cheese around the sides of each plate, and sprinkle the orange pieces, lemon zest, and walnuts over the top. Pour the dressing over the salad, and serve.

Lamb and Lobster

The sophisticate's surf and turf. I love the way this fish and meat dish symbol-izes the flavors of the Mediterranean and the way the two flavors unite on the plate.

> 1 rack of lamb, tenderloin boned out and bones reserved
> Olive oil, enough to baste lamb bones with a pastry brush
> Salt and pepper to sprinkle over lamb bones
> 1 whole lobster, about 1½ pounds
> 2 tablespoons butter
> 2 whole, peeled shallots
> 1 cup chopped ripe tomato
> 1 cup chopped carrots
> 1 cup brandy
> ½ cup heavy cream
> ¾ teaspoon finely chopped rosemary

Preheat oven to 450 degrees. Two hours in advance, baste the lamb bones with olive oil, salt, and pepper and bake for 30 minutes.

Drop the lobster into a pot of 2 inches of steaming water and cook for exactly 12 minutes. Pull the lobster out to rest at room temperature. Reserve the water. Remove the tail and claws from the lobster and wrap the tail and claws in plastic wrap.

Using a cleaver, chop the remaining parts of the lobster and put back into the water. Add the lamb bones. Cook at a high simmer for 20 minutes, then pour the liquid through a fine sieve.

In a sauté pan, heat the butter. Add the shallots and cook until tender. Then add the tomatoes and carrots. Cook for 10 minutes. Add the brandy and lobster–lamb stock and simmer for 5 more minutes. Pour all of the ingredients into a food processor and puree. Slowly add the cream. Add salt and pepper to taste. Reserve the sauce until ready to serve.

Baste lamb tenderloin with olive oil, salt, pepper, and rosemary. Then grill or sauté, turning once, until lamb reaches an internal temperature of 135 degrees. Allow to rest for at least 10 minutes.

While the lamb is resting, remove the plastic wrap from the lobster pieces and remove its tail, leaving it whole: cut down the two sides of the shell, working from the inside, but not cutting into the meat. Kitchen shears work best for this. Crack the claws gently and remove the meat, leaving the claws as intact as you can.

Slice both the lobster tail and the lamb tenderloin into $1/2$-inch medallions so that the pieces look similar. Alternate pieces of lamb and lobster on each plate. Place a claw in a decorative fashion on either end of the plate.

Heat the sauce. Set the oven to 250 degrees and put the plates in the oven only long enough to rewarm but not to further cook the lobster and the lamb. Pour the sauce over the top. Alternatively, place the sauce on the bottom of the plate and the medallions on top of the sauce.

Suggested wine: merlot

Sicilian Cornmeal Cake with Ruby Red Sauce

from Lucy Gore, proprietor-chef, Cafe Lucy's

I've chosen this cake because it embodies the compromise necessary in any successful relationship: It offers the heft and texture to satisfy chocolate cake fans and the almond and vanilla flavors and aromas to make the lover of pound cake or angel food cake happy. It's fragrant and loves a little sweetness on the side. Napa chef Gore serves hers with berries and cream, rhubarb sauce, or poached fruit. I like it with figs and cream or a simple red fruit sauce, which I've included here.

It's called Sicilian cornmeal cake because an intimate friend of Gore's once said, "Now that is a Sicilian cornmeal cake."

1 cup unsalted butter, softened
1 cup plus 1 teaspoon sugar
3 eggs
1 cup toasted and ground almonds
Zest and juice of half a lemon,
½ scant teaspoon almond extract
½ scant teaspoon vanilla extract
⅓ cup flour
½ cup cornmeal (coarse grind gives a better texture, but finer
  will work)
1 teaspoon baking soda

½ scant teaspoon salt
Ruby red sauce (recipe follows)

Preheat oven to 350 degrees. In mixer bowl with whisk attachment, combine butter with sugar and whip at medium speed until fluffy. Add eggs, one at a time, at medium speed, until mixed through. Add almonds, the lemon zest and juice, the almond and vanilla extracts, and mix well. Add flour and cornmeal, baking soda, and salt and mix well.

Line the bottom of a 6-inch round cake pan with parchment (a pan with a removal bottom is best) and spray or coat with vegetable oil. Pour in batter, level the top with a spatula or knife, and bake for 45 minutes to 1 hour. Check by inserting a toothpick in the middle of the cake; when the cake is done, the toothpick will come out clean. Let cool before removing from pan.

To serve, cut the cake and top with ruby red sauce.

Ruby Red Sauce

¼ pound cherries, pitted
3 tablespoons sugar
Squeeze of lemon juice

Cook the fruit in enough water to cover. When the skins pop and the fruit has softened, continue to cook until the fruit turns slightly jammy, then run the fruit through a sieve. Return fruit sauce to a pot with enough sugar to sweeten to taste, heat through, add lemon juice, and serve.

Note: This quick sauce can be made from a variety of ripe red fruits. You can use red plums, raspberries, strawberries, or other red fruits.

Marabout of My Heart

High-yellow of my heart, with breasts like tangerines,
 you taste better to me than eggplant stuffed with crab,
  you are the tripe in my pepper-pot,
   the dumpling in my peas, my tea of aromatic herbs.
    You are the corned beef whose customhouse is my heart,
    my mush with syrup which trickles down my throat.
    You are a steaming dish, mushroom cooked with rice,
    crisp potato fries, and little fish fried brown . . .
    My hankerings for love follow you wherever you go.
    Your bum is a gorgeous basket brimming with fruits
     and meat.

—Emile Roumer

From *Open Gate*, editors Jack Hirschman and Paul Laraque (Willimantic, CT: Curbstone Press, 2001). Reprinted with permission of Curbstone Press.

Almond Love Bites

from Vincent Schiavelli, author and actor

Makes 12 cookies

According to Schiavelli, the Sicilian love affair with almonds has been going on for a thousand years. In many cultures, almonds are linked to spring and to fertility, and almonds, sugar-coated and sometimes colored, are ritually given to guests at weddings and at baptisms. "Almond eyes" always receive a high rating in the looks department.

While these "love bites," which are baked, then cooled, then baked again, may go hot and cold, then hot on you, their sexy texture—chewy on the surface and soft in the center—should get just the right hot reaction from the object of your affections. . . .

4 ounces blanched whole almonds
½ cup granulated sugar
¼ heaping teaspoon honey
⅛ teaspoon almond extract
1 egg white, lightly beaten
Confectioners' sugar for dusting
Flour for dusting hands

Coarsely chop almonds in a food processor by pulsing for several seconds. Add the granulated sugar and continue to process for about 2 minutes, or until the almonds turn into a meal as fine as sugar. Transfer the almond mixture to a bowl, and break up any clumps with your fingers.

In a small bowl, thin the honey with the almond extract. Using an electric mixer fitted with a paddle on low speed, or by hand, thoroughly combine the honey mixture and egg white into the almonds to form a sticky, heavy paste.

Lightly dust a work surface with the confectioners' sugar, and, with hands dusted with flour, form the paste into a ball. Knead it, adding pinches of confectioners' sugar as required, until the paste is cohesive and the surface is less sticky.

Place the paste in a pastry bag fitted with a ½-inch fluted tip. Line a sheet pan with parchment paper and pipe the paste onto the pan in 3-inch squiggles. Place the pan in the refrigerator, uncovered, and chill overnight.

Remove cookies from the refrigerator. Preheat the oven to 300 degrees, and position a rack in the center of the oven.

Bake the cookies for about 20 minutes. Let cool for 10 minutes, and then rebake for an additional 10 minutes. Let the cookies cool to room temperature before removing them from the pan.

Culinary Quickie

Balsamico

Called Italian "black gold," the real balsamico certainly fulfills the criterion of an aphrodisiac being expensive—you won't pay less than $50 for just a few ounces of the real stuff—and you can fork over $500 for the primo stuff (but these are like ancient jewels, with pedigrees going back to 1650, since the barrels in which they are aged can be that old).

Historic Italian gastronomic literature refers to balsamico as far more than just the sublime king of condiments: It is also a tonic, digestivo, liqueur—and an aphrodisiac. There's also something vaguely ecclesiastical, even sacramental, about balsamico. Tasting drops of the revered elixir is akin to drinking a fine old port. The root word "balmsamo," it's conjectured, stems from "balm," as in healing potion.

The real stuff comes from Modena—not from Naples or Florence or anywhere else in Italy that might be listed on the label of a salad–quality balsamic vinegar. Sure, it's just aged grapes, as is any vinegar, but aging something for a minimum of twelve years in the particular wood in which balsamico is aged is what ratchets up the price. While there are excellent quality balsamicos that can rival and cost the same as premium *aceto balsamico tradizionale*, only the latter is decked out with seals and certificates (the pomp and circumstance of Italian law) awarded by a Consorzio and christened as *tradizionale* on its label.

Balsamico was introduced in the United States by that grande dame of the Italian kitchen, Marcella Hazan, who showed us how a sublime drop of balsamico could enhance everything from soups and stews to vegetables and fruits with a subtle and refined note. Balsamico can bless ripe strawberries, elevate vegetables to levels of haute cuisine, and turn a plain salad of fresh greens into something near-miraculous. Use a drop in a salsa or chutney and you enhance the subtle sweet and sour notes. Drizzle a little on vanilla ice cream or Parmesan cheese, eggs, or pasta for a surprising gustatory experience. If your beloved is a dedicated wine lover, it's nearly guaranteed that he or she will be surprised and beguiled by such a gift and will take immense delight in licking it off a ripe strawberry.

The *New York Times* published a recipe imitative of the real stuff a few years ago. While this vinegar admittedly lacks the syrupy texture, depth of character, and complexity of a real balsamico, it is still quite a few steps up from any salad vinegar you'll come across. I have included a larger quantity because this also makes a lovely gift or seduction invitation: "Come, taste some more. . . ."

"Until the Real Thing Comes Along" Balsamico

From Molly O'Neill, "Magic Potions That Stir Food to Life"

Makes 1½ cups

2 tablespoons sugar
3 cups balsamic "salad" vinegar of salad-dressing quality
   (anywhere from $3 to $30)
2 juniper berries, halved
½-inch piece vanilla bean, split
20 needles fresh rosemary
2 black peppercorns
6 raisins
¼ teaspoon dried fig
¼-inch piece dried star anise
1 tablespoon honey
½ teaspoon molasses (optional)
½ teaspoon Worcestershire sauce (optional)

In a heavy-bottom skillet over medium-high heat, simmer 2 tablespoons sugar with 1 tablespoon water until they are dark caramel—
but not burned—2 to 3 minutes. Remove from heat, then add 1 cup
of the vinegar. Lower heat and simmer until the mixture is a very
thick syrup, about 12 minutes.

Carefully add half the remaining vinegar, stirring constantly, and scraping the syrup to incorporate it. Add juniper berries, vanilla bean, rosemary, peppercorns, raisins, fig, and star anise, and continue simmering until liquid is reduced by nearly two-thirds and measures about $1^1/_2$ cups. This will take 20 to 30 minutes.

Add the honey, bring to a simmer, and remove from heat. Cool to room temperature. Taste and adjust the flavor with the molasses (for a darker, caramel tone) or the Worcestershire sauce (to enhance the spice tone). Strain.

6

Carnaval

★ Ceviche with Mango ★
★ Spicy Shrimp on Cilantro Salad ★
★ "Beyond Where the Devil Dropped His Poncho" Peruvian Crab Stew ★
★ Turkey with Mole Sauce ★
★ Rice Pudding with Cherries ★

While the rest of the world may have to cover up to celebrate Carnaval in climates where there might still be snow on the ground, in South America the joyous festival of Carnaval is celebrated by barely clad revelers. The cuisine is much like the culture: spicy, flavorful, a combination of a variety of tastes and colors.

Carnaval has its own rousing traditions, though, and in a place like Venice, when the masks come out the parties rival Rio's in duration, costumes, and celebratory foods.

Ceviche with Mango

Ceviche is synonymous with the spirit of a Mexican or Caribbean vacation: It's a light fish dish that takes as little effort to make as slipping into the turquoise sea for a swim. Use the freshest fish you can find and spice it up with some chiles and cilantro. Ariba!

½ pound small bay scallops or other very fresh fish, such as
    red snapper fillets, skinned and cut into ½-inch pieces
½ cup fresh lime juice
½ mango, peeled and finely diced
1 shallot or ¼ red onion, peeled and finely diced
½ chile pepper, seeded and minced
½ clove garlic, peeled and minced
½ teaspoon coriander seeds, crushed
⅓ cup chopped mint leaves
1 tablespoon chopped fresh cilantro
Salt and pepper

In a small nonreactive (nonmetal) bowl, combine the scallops and lime juice. Cover and marinate in the refrigerator for a minimum of 7 hours, or overnight. The fish should be white and opaque and appear cooked.

Drain the scallops and discard the lime juice. Transfer scallops to a small bowl, add the remaining ingredients, and serve.

I am a shellfish just come from being saturated
with the waters of the Lucrine lake, near Baiaae,
but now I luxuriously thirst for noble pickle.

—Martial Epigrams (ca. A.D. 95)

Spicy Shrimp on Cilantro Salad

Here is a variation of the esteemed food writer Craig Claiborne's curried shrimp that uses cardamom. I love the unusual spin that cardamom gives the dish, and the addition of turmeric gives the shrimp a golden color.

1 pound shrimp
1½ teaspoons turmeric
1½ tablespoons peanut or safflower oil
1 small clove garlic, diced
1 tablespoon sherry
½ small hot red pepper, seeded and finely chopped
1 teaspoon salt
1½ teaspoons diced fresh ginger
½ teaspoon cardamom (or more, depending on preference)
2 tablespoons fresh lime juice
3 tablespoons chopped fresh cilantro
¼ head Boston, Bibb, or other lettuce, washed, dried, and
  shredded (1 cup)

Wash shrimp and sprinkle with turmeric. Add shrimp, cover, and steam until pink, 2 to 3 minutes. When shrimp are cool enough to handle, shell and devein.

Heat oil in a frying pan; when hot, add garlic and cook over low temperature until soft, about 2 minutes. Add shrimp, sherry, red pepper, salt, ginger, and cardamom. Cook until browned, and liquid in pan begins to evaporate, about 3 minutes. Add lime juice. Remove shrimp from pan. Divide lettuce and cilantro between two salad plates, drizzle with pan juices, and top with shrimp. Serve.

Note: A nice alternative to this recipe is to marinate the shrimp for 4 to 5 hours in a mixture of all the ingredients except the lettuce. Then skewer the shrimp on lemon grass stalks or pieces of sugar cane cut into skewers. Quickly grill the shrimp. Pull the shrimp off with your teeth, then suck on the sugar cane.

Suggested wine: riesling or albariño

Many shrimps, many flavors; many men, many whims.

—Malaysian proverb

"Beyond Where the Devil Dropped His Poncho" Peruvian Crab Stew

My friend Linda, a renowned photographer, travels around the world taking hauntingly beautiful photographs. While photographing rock art in Peru, she had "one of the best meals I ever had in my life," prepared for her in a home filled with children and puppies. This stew is a spicy and rejuvenating dish, which may well have something to do with the fecundity apparent in that home.

This dish can be prepared in two stages. The first stage is similar to the base of much Tuscan cooking, such as sauces, soups, and stews, called a "soffritto," which consists of onion, carrots, celery, and olive oil cooked to a roux-like consistency. This recipe is even better the second day when it's thicker and the flavors have melded.

In Peru this dish is often made with crayfish and a wonderful orange chile paste.

½ cup grated yellow onion
2 tablespoons olive oil
1 clove garlic, minced
Pinch of ground clove
Pinch of ground allspice
Pinch of ground nutmeg
Pinch of dried thyme

Pinch of dried oregano
Pinch of cayenne
¼ teaspoon ground ancho chile powder
1 carrot, peeled and grated
1 green bell pepper, seeded and grated
2 small new potatoes, grated
2½ cups chicken stock, heated

6 ounces fresh crab meat
2 tablespoons salsa verde or tomatillo salsa

1 cup medium-diced yellow onion
2 tablespoons olive oil
1 clove garlic, minced
1 red bell pepper, medium dice
1 carrot, sliced thin
2 small red potatoes, small dice
Enough chicken stock to cover vegetables
1 ear fresh corn, kernels sliced off the cob
½ cup fresh or frozen peas
½ cup fresh chopped cilantro
1 Dungeness crab, cooked, cleaned, and cracked
½ cup half-and-half

Using a heavy-bottomed pot, sauté the grated yellow onion in the olive oil over medium heat until soft. Add the minced garlic. Add the spices and herbs, grated carrot, and green bell pepper and increase the heat to medium, cooking until all the vegetables are about half cooked. Stir in the grated potatoes and add enough hot chicken stock to just cover the vegetables. Bring to a boil, then reduce to a simmer for about 30 minutes until the mixture is cooked through and has thickened. Remove from heat. At this point, the mixture can be chilled down and held overnight.

About 2 hours before the stew is to be served, remove the vegetable mixture from the refrigerator and stir in the crab meat and salsa verde or tomatillo salsa.

In a large pot, sauté the diced yellow onion in the olive oil until tender. Add the minced garlic and the red bell pepper and continue to cook for a few minutes. Add the sliced carrot and the diced potatoes with a little chicken stock to moisten, cover and cook for 15 minutes. Reduce the heat to low and stir in the vegetable–crab mixture, corn, peas, and half of the chopped cilantro. Taste and adjust the seasonings. Place the fresh, cracked crab in the pot, pour in the half–and–half, stir, then cover and simmer. In about 15 minutes, check the potatoes for doneness. When the potatoes are cooked through, transfer to a warmed serving dish and garnish with remaining cilantro.

Suggested wine: syrah or grenache

In Baltimore, soft crabs are always fried (or boiled) in the altogether, with maybe a small jock-strap of bacon added.

—H. L. Mencken, *Heathen Days* (1943)

Turkey with Mole Sauce

**Makes 1 quart of mole (use half and
freeze extra sauce for another dinner)**

*Intensely and intriguingly flavored, with an enticing silky sheen, mole is
one of the sexiest of sauces. The combination of different chiles, chocolate,
and cinnamon are what give this dish its complex flavors.*

*While many white or red meats work with mole, this one is made with
turkey. Turkey has a long tradition in Mexico, and in Puebla the streets are
paved with turkey eggs during annual festivities. This recipe uses homemade turkey stock, which is as easy to make as chicken stock is and gives the
dish an authentic flavor. You can use canned chicken stock, but if you're
going to go to the trouble of making a genuine mole, shouldn't you go all
the way?*

The turkey stock (see note):
8 ounces uncooked turkey breast
Extra turkey pieces such as wings or bones (if you have them)
2 carrots, chopped
1 onion, chopped
3 stalks celery, sliced
1 bay leaf
2 or 3 whole cloves
6 to 8 peppercorns
Other vegetable trimmings you have on hand

The mole sauce:
2 ounces mulato chiles, seeded
1 ounce pasilla chiles, seeded
1 ounce ancho chiles, seeded
¼ cup olive oil
1 cup chopped white onion
2 cloves garlic, chopped
2 corn tortillas, shredded
¼ cup raisins
¼ cup almonds, toasted and chopped
2 tablespoons pumpkin seeds, roasted
¼ cup sesame seeds
¼ cup anise seed
2 whole cloves
1 small cinnamon stick
¼ teaspoon black peppercorns
4 ounces canned tomatoes, drained and chopped
4 ounces Mexican chocolate, cut into pieces
1 tablespoon Mexican brown sugar or maple syrup
1 teaspoon sea salt, or to taste

To make the turkey stock, slowly simmer turkey breast and other pieces of turkey with carrots, onion, celery, and water to cover. Bring to a boil, and skim off any foam as it appears. Once the foaming has subsided, add the bay leaf, cloves, peppercorns, and vegetable trimmings (if you have them). Simmer the stock while preparing the mole. When the turkey breast is cooked, remove it from the stock.

To prepare mole, in a large heavy pot, fry the chiles in half of the olive oil, stirring constantly for about 5 minutes. Transfer to a 2–quart saucepan and cover with hot water. Bring to a boil, then reduce the heat and simmer the chiles until they are tender. Drain and set aside.

In the pot in which the chiles were fried, sauté the onions on medium heat until tender and then stir in the garlic. Add the tortillas, raisins, almonds, pumpkin seeds, half of the sesame seeds, the anise seed, cloves, cinnamon stick, peppercorns, tomatoes, and chocolate. Cook for a few minutes and then add the drained chiles and cook a little more.

Place the mixture in a food processor with 1 cup of turkey stock. Pulse to begin and then puree, pouring 2 cups of the turkey stock through the feed tube in a steady stream.

Clean the large pot and return it to the stove.

Heat the remaining olive oil on low and stir in the mole. Thin to the desired consistency using the remaining stock. Simmer for 5 minutes and then add the brown sugar and salt. Taste and adjust the seasoning.

To serve, slice the cooked turkey breast and arrange the slices on a warm platter. Ladle the mole generously over the meat and sprinkle with the remaining sesame seeds. Serve with warm tortillas.

Note: Fresh or canned chicken stock can be substituted for the homemade turkey stock. Poach the turkey breast in the stock, and then reheat the sliced meat in a little of the stock before serving.

Suggested wine: cabernet

Chili's a lot like sex: when it's good it's great, and even when it's bad it's not so bad.

—Bill Boldenweck, *American Way* (1982)

Rice Pudding with Cherries

It's homey and comforting, reminiscent of nursery food, yet it's also seductive. This pudding is a variation of a South American classic, but made like a risotto with Arborio rice and gradual additions of cooking liquid. The rice relinquishes its starch and relaxes into a warm milk bath; the result is soupy, warm, sensual, and bright with red cherries.

    2 cups whole milk
    ½ cup Arborio rice
    ⅛ teaspoon salt
    ½ cinnamon stick
    ¼ pound dried cherries, chopped
    ⅛ cup honey or sugar
    ½ teaspoon vanilla extract
    Ground cinnamon
    Zest of ¼ lemon

Warm the milk. Heat the rice with 1 cup water, salt, and cinnamon stick. Slowly add the warmed milk, just as if you were making risotto, about ¼ cup at a time, stirring constantly. Let most of the milk absorb before each addition. Add the cherries 10 minutes into cooking. After about 17 to 20 minutes, when the pudding is still soupy and you've used up the milk, add the honey or sugar and vanilla.

Take the pot off the heat, pour the pudding into a bowl, remove the cinnamon stick, sprinkle with ground cinnamon and lemon zest, and serve with two spoons.

Culinary Quickie

Tomatoes

Ah, the Love Apple. Its history studded with peccadilloes (as a nightshade it was considered poisonous), it has been considered a dangerous aphrodisiac—even deadly—by various cultures for centuries. "An evil fruit, ... treacherous and deceitful" was how one of its enemies described the tomato as recently as the twentieth century. It was compared to far worse than that by earlier cultures, some of which mistakenly thought it was identical to the mandrake (the mandrake is also known as Satan's Apple). You can thank the French for this buxom red fruit's misnomer "the love apple": It was a faulty translation of *poma amoris, pommo di Moor* (Moor's Apple), or *pommo di amour*. Once southern Italy discovered the tomato, the comely girl with the questionable past was given a proper last name and a wedding ring—and canonical status in the cuisine.

In season, a luscious and ripe tomato acts as the centerpiece to a meal. Canned or in paste form, it is the gracious sidecar to countless Italian sauces. You wouldn't suspect it but many chefs claiming different national origins count on a tablespoon or two of tomato paste (or even ketchup) to add a certain something to their culinary creations.

This chutney recipe works well for winter dishes—it's wonderful with firm-textured fish that has an assertive flavor, as well as a variety of light or dark meats. Try it on hamburgers or lamb burgers for a tantalizing twist.

A Tuscan cook taught me this quick trick for preparing tomatoes for tomato sauce, chutney, or any other tomato dish: Cut the tomato in half and grate it on a large grater, then drain the juice. Good-quality canned tomatoes work just fine if good fresh ones aren't available. Either way, make sure the tomatoes are well drained before cooking.

Tomato-Mango Chutney

1¼ cups seeded, peeled, and drained tomatoes
2 cloves garlic, minced
1 teaspoon grated fresh ginger
¼ teaspoon cumin
¼ teaspoon cayenne
¼ cup honey or brown sugar
¼ cup balsamic vinegar
¼ cup red wine vinegar or fruit-based vinegar
¼ teaspoon salt, or to taste
½ cup sliced mango

Place tomatoes, garlic, and ginger in a medium–size saucepan and bring to a boil. Lower heat and simmer, uncovered, for about 25 minutes, stirring frequently. Add cumin, cayenne, honey or sugar, vinegars, and salt and continue cooking for about 1 hour, stirring frequently, until chutney has thickened.

Add mango and cook for another 5 minutes. Remove from heat and cool. Store in refrigerator for up to 4 days.

7

Late-Night Rendezvous

Maybe you've been working late, out on business, or at a party. But it's late and time to get down to the business of a seductive meal of an avocado soup with velvety appeal, an aromatic pasta and baby peas, a gutsy salad that combines sweet and savory, a burger with gusto from off the beaten track—a meal that finishes with the surprise of a delicate soup spiked with champagne—all fuel for the fireworks to come.

A few of these dishes require advance preparation. Make the chutney, the cardamom meringues, and the soups ahead of time, so that when your mate arrives you can focus on the real business of the day.

Curried Avocado Soup

The avocado's name, shape, and creamy texture all speak to its role as a seductive substance in the aphrodisiac annals. Though its contours are womanly, the Aztecs referred to this fruit as ahuacatl, *meaning "testicle." Its erotic properties were considered so powerful that young Aztec women were forbidden to step outside while the fruit was being harvested. Avocados contain a host of nutrients—perhaps that explains their status as an ancient stimulant.*

Once their rough flesh is receptive to the touch, I personally can find no good excuse not to open one and devour it with a sprinkling of sea salt and lemon juice. If you can get good avocados and are possessed of a little restraint, however, there's no reason not to have a soup this delicious and easy, this smooth and seductive, in the fridge nearly all the time.

Of the two avocado varieties, Floridian and Californian, the latter, being creamier and richer, is generally considered the most desirable.

1 large or 2 small ripe avocados, peeled, pitted, and coarsely
　chopped
1 cup half-and-half
1 to 1½ cups chicken stock
1 tablespoon lemon juice
⅛ teaspoon curry powder
⅛ teaspoon cayenne
⅛ teaspoon cumin
1 teaspoon sherry or cognac (optional)

Salt
2 tablespoons chopped fresh cilantro
Paprika
2 teaspoons salmon roe (optional)

Combine the avocado, half-and-half, chicken stock, lemon juice, curry powder, cayenne, and cumin in the blender. Run at high speed until all ingredients are well blended and mixture is very smooth. Add additional stock if a less creamy soup is desired, and sherry or cognac, if using. Salt to taste. Cover and refrigerate until well chilled.

Divide into two bowls, sprinkle with cilantro and paprika, and pile salmon roe in the center if you are using it. Serve.

Capellini Capriccioso con Piselli

In the Italian kitchen, the word capriccioso *connotes a bit of "fantasia"— and often a dash of whimsy—a dish the cook concocts on the spot in a burst of inspiration. This dish is quick, easy, and satisfies the ravenous. The addition of lemon zest gives the cream sauce a whole other fragrant dimension. Rosemary not only enhances the scent and flavor, but also serves as an aphrodisiac.*

Years ago I read about a variation of this dish in a women's magazine, which advised a girl-on-the-get-go to make this for her man late at night, either before, or after, a rendezvous. I read that it was the perfect sensuous dish, thin strands coated with a light but luscious sauce. I filed it away, as I would a pair of red silk lacy knickers that deserved more frequent outings. Eventually this dish became a seductive staple in my kitchen, as I brought out those lacy knickers more and more.

Whether you use one bowl or two, make sure you do the pasta tango—each of you takes a strand of pasta at its end and then nibbles toward the center.

    1 to 2 tablespoons salt for the cooking water
    ½ pound capellini or cappelli d'angelo pasta (see note)
    1 teaspoon unsalted butter
    1 cup fresh shelled peas or best-quality frozen peas
    2 tablespoons grated Parmesan cheese, plus additional for
        serving
    ¼ cup light cream or half-and-half
    1 tablespoon crème fraîche

½ teaspoon lemon zest
½ teaspoon lemon juice
½ teaspoon chopped fresh mint or ¼ teaspoon dried mint
½ teaspoon finely chopped fresh rosemary or ¼ teaspoon
   dried rosemary
Salt and freshly ground black pepper

Bring a large pot of water to a boil, add salt, and then the pasta. Boil for 3 to 4 minutes (depending on the brand), stirring occasionally until al dente.

While the pasta is cooking, melt butter in a small saucepan, and add the peas. Cover and cook over low heat for another 5 minutes or so, until the peas are tender.

Drain the pasta, saving ½ cup of the cooking water, and return to cooking pot. Add as much of the reserved cooking water, about ¼ cup, as needed, to help loosen the strands of pasta and keep them from congealing. Then add the peas, 2 tablespoons of Parmesan, and the remaining ingredients, and toss with tongs or large serving spoons to coat. Allow the residual heat in the pot to warm the components with the pasta and emulsify the sauce, for up to half a minute.

Serve warm, with a little extra cheese at the table, or bedside.

Note: Cappelli d'angelo (angel hair) is very fine long pasta, and capellini pasta comes curled in a nest shape.

Suggested wine: pinot grigio or pinot bianco

Rocket-in-Your-Pocket Salad

Bitter greens were recommended by Ovis and Martial as sexual stimulants. This salad can be made with any robust green. The combination of bitter greens and salty anchovies is pretty sexy in itself, and this dish couldn't be simpler to make. Put a rocket in his pocket. . . .

- 4 anchovy fillets, drained and finely chopped
- 1 teaspoon lemon juice
- 2 teaspoons extra-virgin olive oil
- 2 cups arugula (also known as rocket), washed, dried, and torn; or any bitter green

To make dressing, place anchovies in a small bowl and mix in lemon juice and then olive oil. Put arugula in a color-complementary bowl and add dressing. Mix with hands. As Elizabeth David said, "I always mix salad with my hands—you need to make sure you feel and coat every leaf."

Lamb Burgers with Balsamico Fig Chutney

When men were asked in a survey what their favorite meat was, lamb was the answer—not steak, pork, or chicken. Think about the falling-off-the-bone richness of a hefty lamb shank, the succulence of a rosy lamb chop, or these plump little patties—and maybe you'll want another pair of hands in the mixing bowl.

½ pound ground lamb
¼ red onion, finely chopped
½ teaspoon minced garlic
½ beaten egg
⅛ cup fresh bread crumbs
1½ teaspoons chopped fresh sage or ¾ teaspoon dried sage
1 tablespoon orange zest, finely chopped
¼ teaspoon paprika
¼ teaspoon cumin
Salt and pepper
4 thick slices crusty country bread such as pugliese or ciabatta
Balsamico fig chutney (recipe follows)
2 lettuce leaves, preferably red oak leaf

Light the grill.

Place ground lamb, onion, garlic, egg, bread crumbs, sage, orange zest, paprika, and cumin in a bowl and mix well. Season with salt and pepper. Form into hamburger patties, and refrigerate until ready to cook.

When grill is hot, cook burgers to desired doneness. Grill the bread slices lightly. Place the burger on a slice of bread, top with balsamico fig chutney, lettuce leaf, and another slice of bread.

Note: Other herbs such as parsley, thyme, or cilantro can be substituted in the burger mix. Lemon or lime zest can be substituted for the orange zest.

Suggested wine: zinfandel

Balsamico Fig Chutney

1½ teaspoons olive oil
2 small shallots, peeled and sliced (about ½ cup)
1 cup dried figs, stems removed and cut into julienne
1 cup port
2 tablespoons balsamic vinegar
Salt and pepper

Heat the olive oil in a pan. Add the shallots and cook over medium heat until they are soft. Add the figs, port, and 1 cup of water. Bring to a boil and simmer gently until all the moisture has been absorbed, approximately 10 to 12 minutes. Add the balsamico vinegar. Season with salt and pepper.

Fruit Cocktail
Pear Champagne

Is there a more romantic place in New York for a tête-à-tête than Café des Artistes? Not for me, in my 20s, sipping champagne and eating speckled quail eggs in the Café's bar, decorated in the 1930s and 1940s with murals of voluptuous females cavorting with abandon.

⅛ cup sugar
⅛-inch-thick slice fresh ginger, the diameter of a quarter
½ perfectly ripe Bartlett, Anjou, or Comice pear, peeled and cored, top half
1 tablespoon Williams pear brandy
Enough good-quality champagne or sparkling wine to top off two glasses

Bring sugar, ¼ cup water, and ginger to a boil in a small saucepan. Stand the pear half upright in the liquid, and cover and simmer until nearly cooked, but just slightly crunchy. Cut the pear half in two. Place each quarter of the pear in a champagne glass.

Divide the brandy between the two glasses and fill with champagne.

Strawberry Champagne Soup with Cardamom Meringues

from Spencer Gray, personal chef

Spencer Gray regularly cooks dinner parties for some of Hollywood's toniest, and he's passionate about cooking. This is his delectable soup: fresh, juicy strawberries coupled with champagne and garnished with mint and meringues.

The meringues are made with cardamom, a prominent ingredient in aphrodisiac recipes in Arab and Indian cultures. In the Arabic love manual The Perfumed Garden, *cardamom is said to incite passion and restore vigor to men. Gray notes that the meringue recipe "yields more than necessary for the strawberry soup, but these cookies make a pleasant little post-coital snack."*

2 pints fresh sweet strawberries, washed and stemmed
¼ cup light corn syrup
¼ cup sugar
¼ teaspoon lemon juice
Pinch of salt
Pinch of ground white pepper
⅓ cup water
2 to 4 cardamom meringues (recipe follows)

1 bottle of good champagne (rosé is best; buy according to
 your preference and budget)
Fresh mint, finely shredded, enough to garnish two bowls

Puree half the berries with corn syrup, sugar, lemon juice, salt, white
pepper, and water. Push through a strainer into a bowl. Reserve
2 beautiful berries for garnish and cut the remaining ones into a
¼-inch dice. Add to strained puree and chill for 2 to 3 hours. Chill
the bowls in which you plan to serve the soup, too.

While soup is chilling, make the meringues. When soup is fully
chilled, stir in about a cup of champagne. Pour remaining champagne into tall flutes.

To serve, ladle about 2 cups of cold soup into a chilled bowl,
float a couple of meringues in it, add the perfect berry you reserved, and sprinkle a little mint on top. Repeat with the other
bowl. Clink glasses, drink, and devour.

Cardamom Meringues

Makes 16 to 20 meringues

½ cup sugar
⅛ teaspoon ground cardamom
Pinch of salt
2 large egg whites
¼ teaspoon vanilla extract

Preheat oven to 300 degrees. Combine sugar, cardamom, and salt in a small bowl. Using an electric mixer, whip egg whites to barely stiff peaks. With mixer running, add sugar mixture slowly and beat in. Add vanilla extract and beat until egg whites are thick and glossy, like a marshmallow cream.

Drop spoonfuls of meringue on a parchment-lined baking sheet and place in the middle of the oven. Reduce heat to 200 degrees and bake about 90 minutes or until the meringues are straw-colored and come off the paper easily. Let cool and then store in an airtight container.

What wond'rous life is this I lead?
Ripe apples drop about my head;
The luscious clusters of the vine
Upon my mouth do crush their wine

—Andrew Marvell (1621–1678)

8

Pop-the-Question Picnic

★ Eggplant "Caviar" ★
★ Red Pepper and Pine Nut Salsa ★
★ Goat Cheese "Truffles" ★
★ Exotic Mango Soup with
Tropical Fruit ★
★ Truffles au Champagne ★
★ Rabbit Pâté ★
★ Panna Cotta ★
★ Succulent Stuffed Strawberries ★

One of the most active volcanoes on earth is found on Stromboli, one of the islands north of Sicily. You wait until twilight, when the mountain is silhouetted by crimson fountains gashing an indigo sky, to start your three-hour climb to the top. At the right time of year on a good night, the eruptions go off several times an hour.

Stromboli is also the name of a Roberto Rossellini film shot on the island. He and Ingrid Bergman, both married to other people, were having an affair, one of the grand and illicit romances of that decade, as a result of which Bergman had a child out of wedlock. There is a famous black-and-white photograph of Bergman on the island, taken by American photographer Gordon Parks. The photo shows Bergman walking away, a harried look on her face, from a group of black-clad island crones casting disapproving glares in her direction.

Stromboli's beaches are covered with volcanic black rock and there is nothing much to do there in the summer except make love, have an early dinner of fresh sardines and spicy tomato sauce with pasta at the "spaghetti lady's," and then make the climb to see the fireworks up close. One night, we brought a bottle of Veuve Cliquot to the top with us and provisions from the "spaghetti lady." That night is my picnic inspiration.

Picnics present prime opportunities for dalliance. The fresh out-doors and fragrances of nature incite appetites and loosen formali-ties and reserve. Certainly Edouard Manet's *Le déjeuner sur l'herbe*, a painting of a nude woman reclining in a grove amidst a group of admiring men, speaks to the pleasures of the great outdoors. But transporting food and serving at the appropriate temperatures are just a few of the myriad concerns when planning an actual foray into nature. My suggestion is to keep it simple:

The Eggplant "Caviar," Red Pepper and Pine Nut Salsa, Goat Cheese "Truffles," Rabbit Pâté, and Succulent Stuffed Strawberries are all ideal outdoors candidates. The Exotic Mango Soup. Truffles au Champagne, and Panna Cotta are best enjoyed outdoors but close to the boudoir at hand–their more delicate texture makes them difficult to transport. If the weather's not cooperating and *au naturale* outside isn't an option, you can still spread your feast out on your or your lover's floor, and warm things up with a fire or your own heat.

Wherever your feast takes place, write your menu on special paper such as papyrus, and name your picnic dishes all kinds of extraordinary things. Who's to know that "Breast of Blushing Nymph" is just a cold chicken breast?

Eggplant "Caviar"

Long considered an aphrodisiac, the eggplant possesses a handsome form, one that rivals the banana in suggestiveness.

What's more, eggplant is versatile: It can be baked, fried, sautéed, stuffed—eaten almost any way except raw. This dip travels well, so it makes an excellent addition to a picnic.

2 medium-size Japanese eggplants or 1 large eggplant
  (see note)
1 teaspoon vegetable oil
1 tablespoon olive oil
1 clove garlic
1 teaspoon lemon juice
1 teaspoon cumin
1 teaspoon paprika (Spanish smoked paprika is best if you
  can find it)
Pinch of cayenne
Salt and pepper
1 tablespoon chopped fresh cilantro
1 tablespoon chopped fresh parsley

Insert a fork into several spots in the eggplants so that they won't explode in the oven. Brush a baking dish with vegetable oil and bake eggplants until soft and collapsible when the skin is pushed in, about 40 minutes. Let cool for about 15 to 20 minutes.

Peel the skin, remove as many seeds as possible, and drain the pulp through a sieve, pressing to extract the juices. Transfer pulp to a blender and add the olive oil, garlic, lemon juice, cumin, paprika, cayenne, salt, and pepper. Blend just until all ingredients are well mixed. Transfer blended ingredients to a serving dish and stir in the cilantro and parsley.

Serve at room temperature as a spread with pita bread or just feed each other a spoonful at a time.

Note: If you use 1 large eggplant, you will need to first slice it in half lengthwise, sprinkle the halves with salt, let them sit 30 minutes, and then rinse the halves well. You do not need to take these extra steps if you use the smaller Japanese eggplants because they contain fewer seeds and are less bitter.

Red Pepper and Pine Nut Salsa

This tasty spread, or a variation of it, is commonplace in many Mediterranean countries such as Greece and Turkey. You can easily adapt it for Italian cuisine by making a pasta sauce out of it: add another tablespoon of olive oil and substitute ½ cup vegetable or chicken stock for the pomegranate juice.

    2 red bell peppers
    2 cloves garlic
    1 red jalapeño pepper, seeds removed
    2 tablespoons pine nuts
    1 teaspoon coriander seeds, crushed
    1 teaspoon cumin
    Salt and pepper
    1 tablespoon lemon juice
    1 tablespoon pomegranate juice, more if needed
    Drizzle of olive oil

Broil the red bell peppers in the oven, turning occasionally, until they are blackened and blistered all over. Transfer the peppers to a paper bag, close it, and when peppers have cooled, remove their skins and seeds.

Process the roasted peppers, garlic, jalapeño pepper, and pine nuts in a food processor for 30 to 45 seconds. Add coriander seeds, cumin, salt, pepper, lemon juice, and enough pomegranate juice to attain desired consistency, then blend until all ingredients are incorporated.

Transfer from the blender to a bowl, and drizzle olive oil on top. Serve with baguette slices.

Take me a turtledove
and in an oven let her lie and bake
So dry that of her you may powder make
Which, being put into a cup of wine,
The wench that drink'st will to love incline.

—Rowlands (early English playwright)

Goat Cheese "Truffles"

These goat cheese balls, with their dusty beige and black coatings, simulate white and black truffles.

> ¼ pound fresh goat cheese, room temperature
> Salt and pepper
> 1½ teaspoons fennel powder (see note; if unavailable, substitute paprika)
> 1½ teaspoons poppy seeds

Place cheese in bowl and season with salt and pepper. Using a small melon scoop or tablespoon, scoop cheese into balls (if using a tablespoon, also use your fingers to roll the cheese into balls). Roll balls in fennel powder and poppy seeds.

Note: Fennel powder has a distinctive and subtle taste and is now available commercially in some grocery stores. If you live in California, you can make your own by harvesting the wild fennel that fills California's fields and lines its highways. Cut stems of fennel that are about 2 feet long and place topside down in paper bags. Leave for a few weeks, shaking occasionally to release powder. When stems are dried out, harvest the powder and discard stems.

The medieval Book of Hours *advocated picnics as a way of celebrating sensuality. The entry "Season of Summer" is attributed to Philippe de Vitry:*

Under the green leaves, on the soft turf beside a chattering brook with a clear spring near at hand, I found a rustic hut set up. Gontier and Dame Helen were dining there, on fresh cheese, milk, butter, cheesecake, cream, curds, apples, nuts, plums, pears; they had garlic and onions and crushed shallots, on crusty black bread with coarse salt to give them a thirst. They drank from the jug and birds made music to cheer the hearts of both lover and lass, who next exchanged their loving kisses.

Exotic Mango Soup with Tropical Fruit

A friend came up with this delicious fruit soup that bursts with tropical fruit flavors to surprise his girlfriend. It combines a variety of exotic fruit flavors and has a creamy texture set off by the finely chopped fruit.

"We began dating in August," he says. "Shortly after that I asked her to join me for the weekend in Hawaii. She arrived at dusk, to a spectacular sunset, and I met her at the airport with a chilled bottle of her favorite wine—a New Zealand sauvignon blanc—that we promptly consumed in the taxi on the way back. I decided to go straight for the kill—dessert!—and prepared this perfect welcome to Hawaii. I think we rivaled the sunset that evening in intensity."

Peel of half an orange
Peel of half a lemon
Peel of half a lime
½ vanilla bean
½ cup freshly squeezed orange juice
¼ cup sugar
2 pieces star anise
2 quarter-size slices fresh ginger
1 stalk lemon grass, smashed (available in Asian markets)
4 kaffir lime leaves (available in Asian markets)
6 coriander seeds
8 mint leaves plus extra sprigs of mint for garnish

1 ripe mango, peeled and chopped, plus half a mango,
   micro-diced
¼ cup lime juice
Pinch of salt
½ cup tropical fruits, micro-diced; fruits can be mango, fresh
   pineapple, Asian pear, Rambuttan (available canned in
   Asian markets), litchi (available fresh in season or canned in
   Asian markets), kiwi, papaya, or passion fruit

Peel the citrus fruits with a vegetable peeler, removing all the bitter white pith from the inside of the peel. Split the vanilla bean.

Combine the first twelve ingredients (from the peels to the mint leaves; do *not* include the sprigs of mint intended for the garnish) in a medium saucepan. Add 2 cups of water and heat on low until the soup is just below a simmer and the sugar is completely dissolved. Remove from heat and let steep for 1 hour. Cool, strain, and chill.

Place 1 mango in a food processor along with the lime juice and salt. Puree, strain, and chill. Gradually add cooked soup base to mango puree until texture is approximately equal to a cream soup. Slowly add lime juice a little bit at a time, tasting the soup after each addition, until soup tastes pleasantly tart but not alarmingly so.

Combine remaining diced half mango and tropical fruits you prefer. Spoon a heaping mound of fruit in the center of one big beautiful bowl. Pour the chilled mango soup around the fruit. Place a small mint sprig atop fruit and serve chilled with large spoons and two straws.

Truffles au Champagne

Truffles: dirty socks or the pungent smell of after-sex? Novelists, kings, courtesans, and gourmands all seem to adore them—pheromones run amok is the general consensus. Dogs and pigs are trained to hunt these fungi; black ones grow in France's Perigord region and Italy's Umbria; the pricier white truffles are found only in Italy's Piedmont.

Here is an old boyfriend's version of a little foreplay. He introduced me to oysters, truffles, champagne—you name it—and I can vouch for this recipe's effectiveness.

"If it's true," he says, "that one of the leading criterion for what makes a food sexy is how expensive it is, then truffles take the cake. Expensive they are—but a little bit goes a long way, and few foods match their pungent, sexy earthiness. I believe that just about anything can be an aphrodisiac," he adds, "it's all in the way it's presented."

Think about presenting the diamond under a truffle or the proposal on one of the "chocolate calling cards" using the bittersweet chocolate truffle recipe in chapter 1. You're outdoors, imagine truffles and their earthy smell in all kinds of places. . . .

> 1 pint champagne
> ½ teaspoon sea salt
> ½ pound fresh black truffles, lightly brushed to clean

Pour champagne into saucepan and bring to a simmer. Add salt and truffles. Let them cook gently for 30 minutes, then drain, cool slightly, sprinkle with salt and pepper, and serve hot on a white napkin.

Keep the champagne sauce and use it as the stock for an exotic sauce.

Here are fruits, flowers,
leaves and branches
And here also is my heart
which beats only for you.

—Paul Verlaine (1844–1896)

Rabbit Pâté

My friend Paolo concocted the perfect romantic picnic. It was on top of the mountain where he lives. He spread a rustic picnic table overlooking the town of Sonoma in California with fine tableware and glassware, wrote a menu, and quickly swept up his bachelor's mess.

He chose every menu entry with an eye to its symbolic relevance. This consisted of oysters (Venus on the half shell), Rabbit Pâté, Pomegranate Champagne Goblet, and for dessert, Eve's Apple (an unadorned whole apple on a beautiful plate), followed by strawberries with drops of ancient and prized balsamico vinegar, which he imports.

Now the girl might not have popped the question during this particular picnic, but let's call it a very successful outing.

> 1 whole rabbit (obtain dressed from your butcher)
> ¼ cup port
> ¼ teaspoon quatre épices (see note)
> ¼ teaspoon salt
> 2 bay leaves
> 4 thin slices smoked bacon
> ½ cup fresh white bread crumbs
> 2 tablespoons milk
> 1 tablespoon olive oil
> 2 shallots, finely chopped
> 1 clove garlic

1½ teaspoons chopped fresh lemon thyme
2 teaspoons lemon juice
Zest of half a lemon
¼ cup chopped pistachios
1 black truffle weighing about ½ ounce, cut in half, or
    2 pieces foie gras, each about ½ ounce (optional)
4 cornichons
2 tablespoons whole-grain mustard (or to taste)
2 teaspoons chopped parsley

Remove the rabbit meat from the bones, coarsely chop it, and place it in a bowl along with the port, quatre épices, and salt. Cover and marinate in the refrigerator for 2 hours.

Place a bay leaf in the center of a 1–cup ramekin. Repeat with another ramekin. Then line the ramekins with the smoked bacon, allowing some bacon to spill over the sides of the ramekin to cover the top of the pâté.

Place the bread crumbs and milk in a bowl and allow the bread to absorb the milk.

Heat the olive oil in a small pan. Sauté the shallot and garlic until soft but not brown.

Add the shallots and garlic to the bread crumbs. Add the chopped lemon thyme, lemon juice, and zest to the bread mixture.

Preheat the oven to 325 degrees. Remove the rabbit meat from the refrigerator and process it in a food processor until the meat is chopped more finely, but it should not have the smooth consistency of chicken liver pâté. Add the bread mixture and pulse to blend.

Transfer the mixture to a bowl, add the chopped pistachios, and mix well. Cook about a teaspoonful of the mixture in a small pan and check for seasoning. If necessary, add more salt or quatre épices.

Drop a spoonful of mixture in each ramekin, and press it down so the pâté fits the ramekin. Add the truffle or foie gras, if using, and then divide the remaining pâté mixture between the two ramekins. Press the mixture into the ramekin and cover with the remaining smoked bacon.

Cover each ramekin with a circle of parchment paper and then foil, and place them in a baking pan of warm water. Bake for 1 hour or until the center reaches 120 degrees. Let the ramekins cool and then remove the foil and parchment coverings. Turn the pâté out on to a plate, cover, and refrigerate until completely cold.

Serve each pâté on an individual plate garnished with cornichons, a dollop of whole–grain mustard, and chopped parsley. Serve with a crusty French baguette.

Note: Quatre épices is a French spice mixture used in soups, stews, and pâtés. The "four spices" are clove, ginger, nutmeg, and pepper, to which other complementary spices are sometimes added. Cinnamon is often substituted for ginger. Use twice as much ginger and nutmeg as pepper and just a dash of clove.

Suggested wine: pinot noir

Panna Cotta

White as snow, with a quivering quality that renders it rather coy, there is something so virginal about this velvety-textured Italian dessert that you expect it to bear a name like "Novice's Flesh." It's easy to make, delicious to eat, and you can come up with your own play-acting scenarios for its consumption.

The glaze:
¼ cup turbinado sugar
1 teaspoon orange juice

The panna cotta:
1⅓ cups heavy cream
1 vanilla bean, sliced in half lengthwise
¼ cup sweetened condensed milk
1 tablespoon turbinado sugar
¼ package unflavored gelatin

To prepare the glaze, in a small saucepan combine the sugar and orange juice with 1½ tablespoons water. Bring the mixture to a steady simmer and cook until it takes on a caramel consistency. It won't be quite as sticky as caramel, but when your spoon meets with some resistance when stirring, the glaze is done. Pour into a brûlée dish or something comparable, ideally 3¾ inches wide by 1 inch high. Refrigerate to set for as long as you refrigerate the panna cotta.

For the panna cotta, combine all of the panna cotta ingredients except the gelatin and heat on low. Whisk the mixture often. Just as it reaches a simmer, very slowly sprinkle in the gelatin. Whisk vigorously to make sure that the gelatin doesn't "clump." Cook until the consistency begins to thicken.

Pour the panna cotta through a strainer into small dishes. Remove the vanilla bean from the strainer, and use a small knife to scrape the remaining seeds into the panna cotta. Discard the vanilla bean pod. Chill the panna cotta overnight or for a minimum of 6 hours.

To serve, run a thin, warm knife around the inside edge of the dish containing the panna cotta. Place the serving plate on top and holding both dishes, flip them over. Drizzle the glaze around and on top of the panna cotta.

Succulent Stuffed Strawberries

This luscious strawberry recipe combines ripe fruit, creamy sweet cheese, and the complex flavors of dark chocolate to create a mouthful of pleasure. It's one of the most delectable dishes you can feed your lover.

> 12 medium to large strawberries; select based on fragrance and taste, not size (!)
> 4 ounces mascarpone cheese
> 4 ounces bittersweet chocolate, the best you can buy
> 2 to 3 tablespoons heavy cream

Wash, dry, and core strawberries. Remove some of the inner fruit, enough to form a small cavity. Stuff with mascarpone, using a small scoop or a teaspoon.

Place chocolate in a double boiler. Add the cream and heat just to the melting point, stirring once or twice. Cool until warm to the touch but don't let it harden.

Dip stuffed end of strawberries into chocolate, and place on waxed paper. If transporting chocolates outside, line a plastic container with wax paper and place strawberries on it in one layer.

Suggested wine: prosecco, an Italian sparkling wine

Fruit Cocktail
Apple Afternoon Delight

This drink will warm up any afternoon or night. The apple, at once so comforting, at once so profane. Is this fruit with the insidious past (think Eve's rock-the-world bite) the same as the goody two-shoes fruit (think American-as-apple pie)? Taste for yourself . . .

14 ounces hard cider
⅛ teaspoon cinnamon
Few grinds of whole nutmeg, or dash of ground
    nutmeg
⅛ teaspoon fresh ginger, finely minced, or
    ⅛ teaspoon ground ginger
2 ounces Calvados (a French brandy made from
    apples)

Heat cider in saucepan and add spices. When warm enough to drink, add Calvados, pour into two mugs, and serve.

9

Veggie Vitality

★ Fennel, Orange, and Olive Salad ★
★ Butternut Squash Soup with Beet
Swirl and Ginger Cream ★
★ French Beans with Radicchio
and Fresh Mozzarella ★
★ Perfect Mashed Potatoes ★
★ Molten-in-Your-Mouth
Chocolate Cake ★

Who says veggies aren't sexy? Eat your words! What about the Creole Love Apple—the tomato? Vegetable dishes adhere to the *Kama Sutra*'s injunction to play it light: "Do not have a stomach full of food and drink."

Here the emphasis is on color, texture, and flavors: brilliant golds, reds, and greens set off with white; creamy, silky textures;

and a mix of sharp, vibrant, sweet, and rich flavors. Vegetables keep your loved one sated but leave plenty of room for Molten-in-Your-Mouth Chocolate Cake.

Thou art like olives;
it is needful to bear thee.

—Arab proverb

Fennel, Orange, and Olive Salad

Fennel has a long history of cultivation and use as a stimulant. All parts of the fennel plant were used to decorate the body during Dionysian festivals, and Hindu love manuals such as the Kama Sutra *recommend fennel to increase sexual vigor. In Mediterranean countries, where fennel is eaten both cooked and raw, it has long been considered a stimulator of the amatory glands, and of course it meets the ancient rule of suggestive shapes having potent powers.*

In India, little dishes of fennel seeds are presented after dinner, which speaks to the vegetable's role as a digestive and a breath freshener.

1 small fennel bulb, cleaned and thinly sliced
1 small frisée, washed, dried, and torn into bite-size pieces
1 blood orange, peeled, cored, and sliced
12 kalamata olives, pitted and halved
1 tablespoon lemon juice
1 teaspoon chopped lemon zest
¼ teaspoon cumin
2 tablespoons extra-virgin olive oil or flax oil
1 teaspoon chopped pistachios
Salt and pepper

Toss together the fennel, frisée, orange, and olives. In a separate bowl, whisk together the lemon juice, zest, and cumin; then add olive oil, pistachios, salt, and pepper. Dress the salad and serve.

Butternut Squash Soup with Beet Swirl and Ginger Cream

One day after making a beet soup, it occurred to me how smashing the two colors saffron and magenta would look together. I made a beet puree thicker than the squash soup, swirled some on top of the soup, and topped it off with ginger cream.

The beet swirl is nothing short of voluptuous. The velvety texture is achieved by using a good quality whole-milk yogurt and baking or steaming instead of boiling the beets. I recommend asking your beloved to close his eyes and open his mouth . . . then feed him a spoonful of beet swirl. Even if he doesn't like beets, I bet this will win him over.

The soup:
1 medium-size butternut squash
½ medium onion, diced
½ teaspoon finely chopped fresh ginger
2 ounces (¼ cup) unsalted butter
1 ripe pear, peeled, seeded, and diced
¼ teaspoon cumin
2 cups chicken stock
Salt and pepper
Generous squeeze of lemon juice

The puree:
2 medium-size beets
4 ounces whole-milk yogurt
2 tablespoons chicken stock
Salt and pepper
4 fresh mint leaves

The cream topping:
½ teaspoon finely chopped fresh ginger
4 ounces crème fraîche

Start by baking the vegetables. Place the beets in a baking dish, add water to about halfway up the beets, cover with aluminum foil, and bake at 350 degrees for about 45 minutes to 1 hour (or steam the beets until tender). Cut the squash in half, scoop out the seeds, and bake at 350 degrees until tender, about 35 to 40 minutes.

To prepare the soup, scoop the baked squash out of the peel. Sauté onion and ginger in butter in a soup pot over medium heat for 2 to 3 minutes. Add squash, pear, cumin, and chicken stock and cook for 15 minutes, until pears are soft. Season with salt and pepper and add a squeeze of lemon juice, to taste.

To make the puree, rub the skins off the baked beets, or peel them. Quarter the beets, then puree them in a blender with the yogurt, adding stock as needed and salt and pepper to taste, until it reaches a creamy, pureed consistency. It should be slightly thicker than the soup. Add mint, pulsing several times.

Prepare the topping by grating the fresh ginger into the crème fraîche.

To serve, divide the soup into two bowls (preferably of a color that complements the squash and beet colors). Make a circular pattern on the soup with the beet puree by using a spoon or a squirt bottle with a wide nozzle. Top with a dollop of ginger cream in the center and serve.

French Beans with Radicchio and Fresh Mozzarella

All beans are sexy when you think about it, in both their external and internal shape: a long pod with a round seed nestled inside. I love the way the warm beans and radicchio in this dish melt the mozzarella a little and form a delicious sauce that is great for dipping. Caramelized onions add depth to so many vegetable dishes and here counter the radicchio's bitterness. It's the kind of aphrodisiac vegetable recipe that satisfies yet keeps a lover hungry for something more.

> 1 tablespoon olive oil
> ⅓ medium onion, thinly sliced
> ½ pound haricots verts (French green beans—harder to find but worth it), tails cut off and cut into 4- to 5-inch pieces
> 2 ounces (¼ cup) chicken broth
> ½ small radicchio, shredded
> Salt and pepper
> ½ pound (1 regular-size container) water-packed mozzarella, diced or shredded
> Few squeezes of lemon juice

Heat medium–size frying or sauté pan, and when hot, add oil. Keep the heat low and add the onion slices, cooking for 20 to 25 minutes to caramelize them (if the heat is too high, they'll start to fry). When the onions are wilted and light brown in color, add the beans and cook, shaking the pan often, for 4 to 5 minutes. Add the chicken stock and cook 2 minutes more. Add radicchio and cook, covered, until soft, about 3 to 4 minutes. Add salt and pepper and remove from heat.

Place mozzarella in a medium-size bowl. Add beans and radicchio mixture and toss, then add lemon juice.

This dish can be served warm or at room temperature.

Note: I sometimes throw a handful of cherry tomatoes into the bowl with the mozzarella before introducing the vegetables—they add a vibrant color and are softened, as is the mozzarella, by the hot vegetables.

Suggested wine: sauvignon blanc

If your wife is old and your member is exhausted, eat onions in plenty.

—Martial (A.D. 40–103)

Perfect Mashed Potatoes

I have always thought of mashed potatoes as the ultimate potato dish, which should be as decadent as possible. That means butter, olive oil, cheese, and salt—used somewhere in excess of moderation but just shy of over-indulgence. At its simplest and quickest, this means adding a dollop of crème fraîche or Gorgonzola dolce to boiled new potatoes, along with a generous helping of butter, a little half-and-half, and good quality sea salt, and mashing them with my grandmother's wooden masher.

But because I also like to dress up potatoes, I think this is the perfect mashed potato dish: creamy mashed potatoes surrounded by a moat of velvety porcini mushrooms and topped with caramelized shallots. Little ears of fried sage leaves add a decorative, delicious, and crunchy touch.

Although the most common method of preparing mashed potatoes starts by boiling raw potatoes, I find baking russets is the easiest way to arrive at tender, flaky potatoes that take well to the mash. If you prefer, you can boil potatoes for this recipe.

    2 large or 3 medium Idaho or russet potatoes
    1½ shallots, peeled and thinly sliced
    ¼ cup plus 2 tablespoons unsalted butter
    1 tablespoon olive oil
    ¼ pound fresh porcini mushrooms, brushed, caps removed,
        and thinly sliced
    ¼ cup vegetable broth or dry white wine

½ tablespoon kosher or coarse-grained sea salt plus
   additional to taste
¾ cup whole milk
2 scallions, ends and tops trimmed
1 tablespoon crème fraîche plus 1 tablespoon heavy cream,
   or 2 tablespoons heavy cream
Pepper, freshly ground
Dash of freshly ground nutmeg

The garnish:
Olive oil for frying
6 whole fresh sage leaves
Coarse salt for sprinkling

Preheat the oven to 400 degrees. Wash the potatoes and bake them
for about 1 hour, until they are very tender when pierced with a
fork. (Potatoes can alternatively be boiled and peeled.)

While the potatoes are baking, prepare the shallots and mushrooms. Sauté shallots over very low heat in 2 tablespoons of butter
until softened and caramelized, 10 to 15 minutes. In a separate pan,
heat the olive oil and add the mushrooms and the broth or wine
and cook over low heat, covered, for about 10 minutes. Remove
cover and cook until sauce thickens enough to coat a spoon. Add
salt to taste.

About 15 minutes before the potatoes are done, heat the milk
in a medium-size saucepan over low heat, and add scallions, steep-
ing them, never letting the milk approach a boil or simmer. Take

the pot off the heat, remove and discard the scallions. When the potatoes are done, take them out and turn the oven down to 200 degrees. Put the dish in which you plan to serve the potatoes in the oven.

Cut the potatoes open and push them through a ricer or coarse sieve into the pot of heated milk. Use a large wooden spoon to beat in the cream, ¼ cup butter, ½ tablespoon of salt, pepper, and nut-meg. Break up the potatoes as you beat, and adjust the liquids and seasonings as necessary.

Transfer the mashed potatoes to the heated serving dish, cover, and place in the oven.

To prepare the garnish, pour olive oil in a small skillet until the oil is ⅛ inch deep. Use moderately high heat to get the oil hot but not smoking. Fry the sage leaves, one at a time, about 3 seconds each, until crisp. Use a slotted spoon to transfer each leaf to paper towels to drain. Sprinkle sage leaves with coarse salt.

Mound potatoes on each plate. Top with caramelized shallots. Arrange the mushrooms and their sauce in a ring around the pota-toes. Insert 3 sage leaves at an angle around the top of each portion. Serve immediately. (If covered with foil and kept warm over a pan of warm water, potatoes can be kept for up to 30 minutes.)

Suggested wine: merlot

My idea of heaven is a great big mashed potato and someone to share it with.

—Oprah Winfrey

Molten-in-Your-Mouth Chocolate Cake

This cake could be baked in two ramekins, but why not bake it instead in a 6-inch round or square soufflé dish so that you can eat out of the dish together?

4 ounces bittersweet chocolate, chopped
1 large egg
1 large egg yolk
¼ cup sugar
⅓ cup unsalted butter plus extra for buttering soufflé dish
⅓ cup flour
Crème fraîche or whipped cream for topping

Preheat the oven to 375 degrees. Butter the soufflé dish. Heat chocolate in a small, heavy saucepan over low heat, stirring gently until melted and smooth.

Blend egg, egg yolk, and sugar in a medium-size metal bowl. Set bowl over a saucepan of barely simmering water (be sure to use a bowl that sits over the water and doesn't touch it) and whisk until just warm to the touch. Remove bowl from over the water. Using an electric mixer, beat egg mixture until very pale, thick, and doubled in size. Incorporate ⅓ cup butter and mix until smooth.

Fold chocolate mixture into egg mixture. Sift flour over the combined mixture and gently fold together. Empty batter into buttered soufflé dish.

Put soufflé dish into oven and bake until tester inserted in the center comes out clean, about 13 minutes. Cool to room temperature, or wait until barely warm, but not hot, to garnish with crème fraîche or whipped cream. Dig in.

Culinary Quickie

Onions

It's not only those foods that have suggestive shapes or colors or that are scarce that have been thought of as seductive. Greeks, Romans, Arabs, and Hindus—all emphatically pronounced the onion an aphrodisiac and coital aid. Ancient Greece's most favored Viagra, onions are also frequently used in Roman and Arab recipes. The sixteenth-century erotic treatise *The Perfumed Garden* makes no bones about the onion's priapic powers:

> *The member of Abou el Heioukh has*
> *remained erect*
> *For thirty days without a break because he did*
> *eat onions.*

Onions are also mentioned numerous times in the *Kama Sutra* and other Hindu love-instruction manuals. Some ancient Hindu recipes recommend adding honey to onions; others advise mixing onions with egg yolks; if eaten for three days, one text advises, the result is "an energetic stimulant toward coitus."

Onion and garlic contain the amino acid alliin, an interesting compound absent of odor or taste until it is crushed—then the enzyme allinase kicks in and converts alliin into allicin—releasing the pungent aromas packed into these powerful bulbs, as well as antibiotic properties. To mellow sharp onions, rub salt into raw slices and let them sit for 5 minutes, then rinse and pat dry.

An Italian chef in New York whose family owns several restaurants was once giving a demonstration in his kitchen to the New York Women's Culinary Alliance. He began slicing onions, fast as lightning, then stopped and put his knife down. "My mother," he said, with a confessional grimace, "I love her, but she starts all her recipes with garlic." He shrugged. "I start mine with onions."

It was years later when that fundamental difference made sense to me. As much as I love garlic and believe in its medicinal and aphrodisiacal properties, a caramelized onion—silky in texture, sweetly complex in taste—is the way I prefer to start many of my recipes, too.

There is a world of difference between cooked onions and caramelized onions. I use caramelized onions as the start of numerous pasta sauces and vegetable dishes such as ratatouille. Slicing onions thinly and cooking them at a low temperature turns them silky and voluptuous and gives them a depth and complexity of flavor that quick- or stir-fried chopped onions just can't match.

Caramelized Onions

2 tablespoons olive oil
1 tablespoon butter
3 medium onions, thinly sliced
½ teaspoon finely chopped rosemary
Dash of white pepper
1 clove garlic, finely chopped
¼ teaspoon brown sugar
1 tablespoon cooking-quality balsamic vinegar

Heat pan (or two pans, as needed to fit onions in one layer), add oil and butter, and when they are hot, add onions, rosemary, and white pepper. Cook at very low heat for about 20 minutes, stirring lightly occasionally. Add garlic and brown sugar and continue cooking about another 15 minutes. Add balsamic vinegar and cook until onions are brown and caramelized, about another 5 minutes.

Either use immediately as called for in a recipe, or let cool and refrigerate for later use.

10

Tying the Knot

The guests are gone, the vows are made, the honeymoon's over—but not yet! Whether you have just returned from the day's nuptial festivities or your honeymoon, now is the moment when you are about to embark on your married life together. Make this your first meal of celebration.

It should be reflective of new and old, of ancient symbols of rejuvenation, and of tried-and-true foods that stimulate appetite of more than one kind. If this is your second time around, reflect on the elements of these dishes that use surprise to keep cooking and dining together fresh and fun. Consider how certain combinations and contrasts speak to the compromises required in any good marriage. Look to your meals together as a time to appreciate each other anew and to lend a helping hand where needed. Consider the kitchen the first place where you want your mate to really listen and pay attention to you; the bedroom, of course, is the second.

I stick to asparagus, which seems to inspire gentle thoughts.

—Charles Lamb, *Essays of Elia* (1823)

Champagne Terrine

What drink is more male than a pint of dark, bitter Guinness, and what drink more female than a fizzy glass of champagne? This liquid terrine brings together the yin and yang—Guinness, touted in Ireland for its aphrodisiac properties, with the most delicate and elegant of drinks, champagne. In the 1970s in Ireland, a Champagne Terrine was advertised in magazines as Black Velvet. Irish women have traditionally drunk Guinness with cassis to sweeten the bitterness, much like a shandy.

It may seem a travesty to both drinks to mix them but they make wonderful partners. The bitterness of the chocolaty malt and the sweetness of the champagne offset each other perfectly. The drink separates into two beautiful layers—the Guinness's silky, creamy head topping the prickle and pop of the semisweet champagne's bubbles. It's great to serve with freshly shucked oysters and delicious with the Cheese Love Knots.

1 bottle champagne, demi-sec or doux, chilled
1 can draught Guinness, chilled

Fill two champagne flutes halfway with champagne and allow the foam to subside a little. Slowly add the Guinness to the flutes to form two distinct layers.

Cheese Love Knots

Makes 24 twists, enough for freezing half for later

These rich cheese twists are a great love snack. They can be baked in advance, then once they have completely cooled, frozen and reheated before serving. Excellent served with drinks, such as the Champagne Terrine here, Cheese Love Knots also make a sweet little gift or stocking stuffer for your beloved.

½ cup flour
1 teaspoon baking powder
Pinch of dry mustard
Pinch of salt
¼ cup (½ stick) butter
⅓ cup grated sharp yellow Cheddar cheese
1 egg, lightly beaten
2 tablespoons sweet paprika

Preheat the oven to 350 degrees. In a large mixing bowl, sift to-gether flour, baking powder, dry mustard, and salt. Combine this mixture with the butter and cheese in the bowl of a food processor and pulse to make a coarse meal. Add the egg, pulsing until dough becomes thick and pasty.

On a lightly floured surface, roll out the dough to about ¼-inch thickness, then cut into 5-inch or 6-inch long strips (or use a cookie cutter to make hearts or other shapes instead of strips). Twist the strips, sprinkle lightly with the paprika, and place each strip 1 inch apart on a greased cookie sheet. Bake until golden brown, about 15 minutes.

Cover tightly with plastic wrap and store in an airtight container for up to 5 weeks.

Bread has long been connected to sex and fertility. A German description of a wheat ritual dating back to sometime in the eleventh century entails a woman undressing and rolling around in harvested, but unthreshed, wheat. After the wheat was threshed, she used this flour to make "love bread." Any man eating the bread would immediately desire her. The Italians have a bread called capiette, *which resembles a couple having sex, perhaps referencing the ancient traditions of copulation in wheat fields in order to ensure the field's fertility.*

Asparagus in Bed

Even the spear shape of the asparagus (which is a member of the lily family) suggests its power as an aphrodisiac. Historically, the Greeks grew it, the Arabs sprinkled it with condiments that enhanced its aphrodisiac properties, and the Chinese used it as a remedy for infertility. Seventeenth-century French royalty believed in its boost, and why not: Asparagus contains a lot of protein for a vegetable and is high in B vitamins, folic acid, and the nutrient asparagine, key for prostate health. The Arab text The Perfumed Garden *suggests that a man "do it quicker than you can cook asparagus"!*

Certainly the plant's proclivity to multiply has something to do with its claim to sexiness. And perhaps its rapid ascent: It's said that a spear can grow as quickly as 10 inches in 24 hours.

As with many asparagus recipes, my friend Leslie's starts with steaming and ends up with eggs, long associated with fertility and rebirth. An energetic red-headed American who is a long-time resident of Venice, Italy, Leslie's beautiful studio full of Murano glass jewelry is right on the Grand Canal. If you were her boyfriend Michele, you could wave to her from the vaporetto (the Venetian public bus system consists of motorboats) as it pulled up in front of her dock and be invited inside for this delicious dish. She made this for Michele on their first date, which she reports was highly successful.

3 eggs
1 pound fresh asparagus, bottoms and rough edges
   trimmed off
1 tablespoon extra-virgin olive oil
Salt and pepper
2 tablespoons finely grated Parmesan cheese

Put unshelled eggs in a small pot of cold water and bring to a boil. Reduce heat to simmer. Remove two of the eggs in about 3½ minutes, and place them in a bowl of cold water to arrest cooking.

Boil the remaining egg for an additional 8 to 10 minutes. (Cooking time will vary, depending on the size of the egg. If the eggs are just out of the refrigerator, add another 2 minutes to the cooking time.) Remove egg from pot and place in cold water.

Steam asparagus until just tender, 3 to 5 minutes. While asparagus are steaming, break up and whisk the 2 medium-cooked eggs with the olive oil, salt, and pepper.

When the asparagus are cooked, arrange them on a platter and blanket them across the middle with a thick band of the egg mixture. Halve the remaining hard-boiled egg and place each half on an end of the asparagus band. Sprinkle Parmesan over the asparagus and serve at once at room temperature.

Suggested wine: prosecco or gewürztraminer

Golden Roasted Potatoes with Rosemary

The history of the much-maligned spud is a mixed one. *Early gossip and hearsay referred to potatoes as "testicles of the earth" when they were first brought to Europe from Peru (where they are, and were, integral to culinary customs). It took a while before potatoes were embraced as an aphrodisiac. They were more likely to be reviled as poisonous nightshades, a status relegated to a sister nightshade, the tomato. The English associated the potato with the lusty and fecund Irish. Shakespeare got it right in* The Merry Wives of Windsor, *though:*

> *. . . let the skies rain potatoes/kissing comfits . . .*

Outside of mashed potatoes, my favorite potatoes are wedges coated with olive oil and rosemary, sprinkled with salt, and then roasted until they have a crispy, salty exterior and creamy interior. Golden and fragrant, they are delicious with just about anything and at any meal or as a love snack.

¼ cup extra-virgin olive oil
6 cloves garlic, peeled and crushed
1 pound yellow potatoes, such as Yukon gold, peeled and cut
  into small wedges
2 tablespoons chopped fresh rosemary
Sea salt (lavender salt is nice if you have it) and pepper

Preheat the oven to 425 degrees and set a medium–size pot of water on to boil.

Warm the olive oil over low heat in a medium–size baking pan on the stovetop and add the garlic. When the garlic begins to sizzle and becomes fragrant, about 20 seconds, remove from the heat.

When the water boils, add the potatoes for about 12 seconds, then transfer them to the baking pan using a slotted spoon. Add rosemary, salt, and pepper, and toss to coat.

Reduce the oven heat to 375 degrees. Put the potatoes in the oven and roast them for about 45 minutes to 1 hour, until they are golden and crispy. Turn them several times so that they don't stick to the pan.

Serve while hot.

Poached Salmon with Orchids

The orchid—so beautiful and seductive, so manipulative. The orchid attracts male insects such as flies by releasing pheromones duplicating those of the insect's female species, and the male flies try to copulate with the flowers. Eventually they stomp out, frustrated and unsuccessful, but carrying with them pollen grains from the orchid. No one said male flies are smart, but nature is: The next time the flies try to make it with an orchid, they transfer the pollen of the first, effectively pollinating the flower.

The orchid used as decoration here is cymbidium, an edible flower, but one best used as a garnish.

2 salmon steaks, each weighing 6 to 7 ounces
Salt and pepper
2 cups dry rosé or white wine
1 bay leaf
5 black peppercorns
½ teaspoon salt

The sauce:
1 egg yolk
1 clove garlic, minced
1 teaspoon lemon juice
½ cup olive oil
½ cup safflower oil
½ teaspoon grated orange zest

1 teaspoon chopped fresh dill
Salt and pepper

The garnish:
A spray of cymbidium orchids

Preheat the oven to 375 degrees. Season the salmon well with salt and pepper and set aside.

Put the wine, bay leaf, peppercorns, and salt in a pan large enough to hold both salmon steaks. Bring to a boil and then add the salmon. Simmer gently for 5 minutes and then turn the steaks to cook on the other side for another 5 minutes. The flesh should part easily and be a very rosy pink in the center.

In the meantime, make the sauce. Place the egg yolk in a small bowl. Whisk until pale yellow. Add the garlic and lemon juice and whisk to blend. Mix the olive oil and safflower oil together and then whisk them into the egg yolk–lemon juice mixture, at first a drop or two at a time and then in a steady stream Add the orange zest and chopped dill. Season with salt and pepper to taste.

Remove the fish from the poaching liquid and place on a platter. Lift the skin off the body. Garnish with the spray of cymbidium if it is a well–shaped spray, or remove the flowers and garnish the platter with individual flowers. Pass the sauce separately.

Suggested wine: pinot noir

Double-Delight Chocolate Pudding Cake

Makes 3 servings, one for later . . .

This dessert is perfect for a marriage celebration because it has two sides: not all pudding, not all cake—it's a happy marriage of the two. It embodies the yin and yang of marriage in each creamy, dense, and delicious bite.

The pudding layer:
8 ounces heavy whipping cream
1 ounce semisweet chocolate, finely chopped
¼ cup sugar
2 large or 3 small egg yolks

The cake layer:
2½ ounces bittersweet chocolate, finely chopped
3½ tablespoons unsalted butter
2 eggs
2½ tablespoons sugar

To prepare the pudding layer, preheat the oven to 300 degrees. Pour the cream in a saucepan and bring to a boil. Remove from the heat.

Place the chocolate in a small bowl. Pour the hot cream over the chocolate and stir until chocolate is melted.

Whisk together the sugar and egg yolks until blended. Slowly add the chocolate mixture to the egg–sugar mixture.

Pour into three 8-ounce buttered ramekins, filling no more than halfway. Place the ramekins in a $9\frac{1}{2} \times 13$-inch baking pan and add hot water to halfway up the sides of the ramekins. Place pan in oven and bake 45 minutes or until pudding jiggles but is lightly set. Cool completely.

To make the cake layer, preheat the oven to 325 degrees. Melt the chocolate and butter in a heavy pan set over very low heat, or in a microwave.

Use an electric mixer to whip the eggs and sugar on high speed until lemon yellow. While still mixing, pour in the chocolate–butter mixture and mix until all ingredients are blended.

Pour the batter over the cooled pudding layer in the three ramekins. Place ramekins in the $9\frac{1}{2} \times 13$-inch baking pan. Add hot water to halfway up the sides of the ramekins and bake for 30 to 40 minutes, or until a toothpick inserted in just the cake layer comes out clean.

Serve warm with honey or vanilla ice cream or chilled.

Culinary Quickie

Nonna Acqua

Succulent, moist foods are seductive, and they get that way, as do humans, through the addition of moisture. The simple secret of chefs and Italian grandmas is liquid lubrication. Those small saucepans you see chefs frequently dipping a ladle into? Generally filled with weakly flavored broths, this is what I call *nonna acqua* (grandma water), liquid nourishment for your recipe,

Wine, in addition to being used for deglazing and in stews, is an excellent liquid to use, but take care that its flavor doesn't over-whelm the food's flavor. I find adding red wine to greens such as spinach or kale just after they've wilted, and covering the pan, adds a sweetness and depth of flavor.

11

Rekindle the Flame

★ Crabmeat Gazpacho ★
★ Spaghetti Light-My-Fire with
Anchovies and Artichokes ★
★ Peach and Pancetta Salad ★
★ Grilled Pork Tenderloin with
Mango-Fig Chutney ★
★ Soft Sexy Grits ★
★ Warm Cherries and Cream ★

The kids are out for the night. You've just managed to complete that blockbuster project—a major success. Whatever the occasion to celebrate, lock the doors and get into the kitchen.

The best thing about rediscovering your love object is the familiarity factor. You know his thinking, you know his nooks and crannies. It's a lot easier to pleasantly surprise someone when you know what he or she likes. This is a chance to try your hand at dishes that are lusty and satisfying and that have a humorous kick to them. Nothing too complicated here, nothing too unknown.

Try trading roles: If he usually cooks, let him serve you in those ridiculous chile pepper silk shorts you bought him in New Mexico . . . or wearing nothing but an apron. If you're usually at the stove, switch over to the proverbial French maid outfit or something more provocative in which to serve cocktails or dessert, if you get that far.

Crabmeat Gazpacho

My friend Maggie says this recipe earned her the title of "Queen of Gazpacho." It is a surefire hit and several steps above your ordinary "uncooked" tomato soup with veggies. The Bloody Mary mix ratchets the gazpacho up a notch and the crab gives it a signature twist.

This soup is best made a day in advance.

3 very large tomatoes, preferably of 3 different colors
1 English cucumber
1 green pepper
1 tablespoon finely chopped red onion
1 ear white corn, grilled (preferably) or steamed
1 tablespoon champagne vinegar
1 tablespoon finely chopped parsley
3 tablespoons very good quality extra-virgin olive oil
¼ teaspoon finely ground chipotle pepper or cayenne
Juice of 1 lime
1 cup Bloody Mary mix, any brand
Salt and pepper
¾ pound jumbo lump crabmeat

Finely chop all the vegetables (except the corn) into the smallest pieces you can. After you have cooked the corn, cut the kernels off the cob.

Place all of the ingredients except the crabmeat into a food processor that is fitted with a stainless steel blade. Gently pulse the ingredients together but don't let them become completely pureed—turn the food processor on and off very quickly while processing to monitor the soup's texture. Chill the soup.

Clean the crabmeat but try to leave the lumps intact. Keep refrigerated until ready to serve.

To serve, pour the chilled soup into brightly colored bowls and top with crabmeat.

In New Orleans, food is like sex. Everybody's interested.

—Ella Brennan, *Travel & Leisure* (1989)

Spaghetti Light-My-Fire with Anchovies and Artichokes

My childhood friend Bob, who grew up to be a hell of a cook, reports that this recipe has always served him well in romantic situations.

If you can find fresh anchovies packed in salt or oil at an Italian or Spanish market they will need to be deboned and filleted, but it's well worth the effort. Just cut off the tails and tops and fillet as you would any fish: Slice it down one side, remove the backbone, and separate the meat into two fillets. Larger than their jarred brethren, fresh anchovies are whiter in color, with a rosy hue, meaty texture, and more flavor.

This, like many of the best pasta recipes, is easy, quick, tasty, and toothsome. The combination of salty anchovies, tangy artichoke hearts, lemon zest, and the fire of red chile pepper stimulates appetites of more than one kind.

> ½ tablespoon olive oil
> ½ tablespoon butter
> ¼ teaspoon salt
> ½ teaspoon brown sugar
> ½ large yellow onion, cut in half pole to pole and thinly sliced
> Black pepper
> ½ pound spaghetti
> 2 cloves garlic, finely chopped
> 2 fresh anchovies, cleaned, deboned, and filleted, or 1 can
>   flat anchovy fillets

1 jar (4 ounces) artichoke hearts, drained and rinsed
1 teaspoon lemon zest
1 small chile pepper such as serrano, seeded and finely
    chopped, or cayenne to taste

Heat a medium-size frying pan to low heat, add olive oil and butter, and when hot, add salt and sugar, then onions. Sauté until they begin to caramelize, about 10 minutes. Add black pepper and about a teaspoon of water.

Bring 3 quarts of salted water to a boil. Put the pasta in the boiling water.

Add garlic to onions and sauté another 5 minutes. Add anchovies and sauté 5 minutes more, until the anchovies start to lose shape and melt into the sauce. Add the artichoke hearts, lemon zest, and chile pepper or cayenne and sauté another 5 minutes.

Drain pasta, then return it to the pot. Add the sauce, toss well, and cook 2 to 3 minutes. Serve.

Suggested wine: verdicchio

Peach and Pancetta Salad

One day my curious companion, who doesn't cook, was routing around in the cabinets for something and came across a bottle of Ume plum vinegar. "What's this?" he wanted to know. I had forgotten about that bottle, like so many other intriguing sauces and condiments we come across in specialty markets and never use.

I considered the vinegar's unusual flavors—strong, sour, and salty—and made this summer salad to complement them. The salad touches on all the tongue's tasting zones: sweet, bitter, sour, and salty, to which the Japanese add a fifth, umami, which is a recognition of savoriness. It is also the Japanese philosophy of, you might say, "ripeness is all," that everything, including everything we eat, arrives at a peak moment of realization, of completion, of ripeness. It's like Spaulding Gray's "perfect moment," that brief, fleeting wave that you can ride for just a second before it's gone. Not unlike the touchdown of sex.

The salty pancetta is accented by the sweet corn—and what is more emblematic of sweetness and summer? Well, maybe a peach's sweet, sticky juices running down faces and fingers.

This salad can be doubled to serve as a main course.

    1 teaspoon oil for frying, preferably olive oil
    ¼ pound pancetta
    1 ear corn on the cob
    1 peach, ripe and preferably white, peeled, cored, and sliced

2 tablespoons extra-virgin olive oil
1 tablespoon Ume plum vinegar (available in specialty, Asian,
　　and health food stores, or through mail order) or lemon juice
¼ teaspoon coarse sea salt
Handful of frisée, washed and dried
Handful of arugula, washed and dried

Heat a skillet to medium heat. Add 1 teaspoon of oil, and when it is hot, add the pancetta. Cook until lightly browned, about 8 to 9 minutes. Remove pancetta to a plate lined with paper towels.

Shuck corn, scrape kernels off, and add to the pan. Cook until kernels are cooked though and lightly toasted, about 4 to 5 minutes. Remove, using a slotted spoon.

Add peach slices to the pan, lower heat to medium–low, and cook for 15 to 20 minutes, stirring occasionally, until the slices are very soft. Set aside to cool.

Whisk olive oil into vinegar or lemon juice and salt.

Place pancetta, corn, and peaches in a medium–size serving bowl. Add frisée, arugula, and dressing and toss well.

Saying "She's a real peach" hasn't lost its appeal. The Chinese and Japanese celebrate peach blossoming just as they do cherry flowering, and brides still wear peach blossoms in their hair as signs of fertility. Considered magical flowers, peaches have long been a symbol of virginity and feminine sensual beauty.

Grilled Pork Tenderloin with Mango-Fig Chutney

I love to pair this flavorful pork tenderloin recipe with the recipe for grits that follows. The combination is a Southern classic that translates well into "the best way to a man's heart. . . ." The pork needs to marinate at least 12 hours, so be sure to get into the kitchen early.

The marinade and meat:
½ cup apple cider
½ cup pineapple juice
1 teaspoon ground star anise
¼ teaspoon ground clove
1 bone-in pork loin weighing 3 pounds, preferably organic

The chutney:
4 slices applewood smoked bacon, finely diced (easier if you
    freeze it, then cut it)
1 Vidalia onion, medium-dice
12 black mission figs, tops removed, sliced into quarters, or
    dried apricots (see note)
2 ripe but firm mangoes, diced into ½-inch pieces, or pears
    or apples
¼ cup apple cider
¼ cup pineapple juice

1½ ounces (3 tablespoons) bourbon
Salt and pepper
½ to 1 teaspoon honey

Mix all marinade ingredients, except the pork. Then pour the marinade in a plastic bag that seals tightly, add the pork, and refrigerate. Turn the plastic bag every 6 hours, and marinate the pork for 12 to 24 hours.

To prepare the chutney, heat a medium–size sauté pan until it is fairly hot. Then add the bacon, reduce the heat to low, and cook until all of the fat is released and the bacon is crispy.

Add the onion and cook until it begins to turn translucent in color.

Add the figs and the mangoes. Cook for about 15 minutes or until all of the ingredients are well integrated.

Increase the heat to medium. As the ingredients begin to boil, add the juices, bourbon, salt, pepper, and honey. Cook for another 5 minutes and then remove from the stove. The chutney can be served warm, cold, or at room temperature.

Before lighting your grill, spray oil or pour a few drops of oil on each piece of the cooking area, then use a paper towel to rub the oil over the surface; this will keep the pork from sticking.

Light the grill, and when it is at an even medium heat, drain off the marinade from the pork. Cook the pork, turning it every 4 minutes or so, until it reaches an internal temperature of 145 degrees. Then set it aside to "rest" for a full 10 minutes. (It will keep cooking

on its own and will be twice as moist if you don't skip this part of the procedure.)

To serve, slice the tenderloin into diagonal medallions. Fan the pork slices out on the plate (they are great when served over the grits recipe that follows). Generously spoon chutney and its liquid on top of the pork.

Note: Ancients such as Apicus recommended apricots with pork. The fruit's deeply sweet and tart flavor, when dried, complements the pork beautifully.

Suggested wine: viognier

There is a garden in her face,
Where roses and white lilies grow;
A heav'nly paradise is that place,
Wherein all pleasant fruits do flow.
There cherries grow, which none
may buy . . .

—Thomas Campion (1567–1620)

Soft Sexy Grits

from Jan Birnbaum, chef-owner, Catahoula's

Makes enough for 2 servings plus leftovers

Award-winning chef Jan Birnbaum, Louisiana-born and bred, cut his chops at establishments like San Francisco's Campton Place before finally opening his own restaurant, Catahoula's, in Calistoga, California, where he can cook the spicy Louisiana food he knows and loves.

"Grits are a staple of the southern cook," says Birnbaum. "They are cooked with water, salt, and butter for breakfast. Some add brown sugar or honey. The leftovers from breakfast are often kept, cooled, and fried later for dinner. These grits are more savory than most and are great with a pork chop or short ribs at dinner. Once you eat them you'll know why we call them 'sexy.' If someone asks why you call them sexy, the answer is 'Because I made them.'"

All I know is that every time I have something like Jan's Red Gravy and Grits at Catahoula's, I just want to hustle down to the dance floor of the New Orleans Rock 'n' Bowl and get naughty . . .

6 tablespoons butter
2 cups chicken stock
⅔ cup heavy cream
½ teaspoon chopped garlic

Salt and pepper
1 teaspoon tabasco
⅔ cup Alberts grits or other standard quick grits or ground
    hominy (see note)

Bring butter, stock, cream, garlic, salt, pepper, and Tabasco to a boil. Lower to a simmer and allow the garlic to soften in flavor. The liquid should taste overseasoned at this point. (Remember that the grits will absorb a lot of seasoning.)

Add the grits, whisking and stirring constantly, and keep at a simmer. As the mixture thickens, remove the whisk and stir frequently with a wooden spoon. Taste for seasoning and texture.

Cook gently until the gritty meal becomes soft and sexy, about 10 to 15 minutes. Keep the grits over a double boiler until ready to serve.

Note: If you can get freshly ground grits, use them. The cooking time for fresh grits is considerably longer, probably twice as long. And because of the longer cooking time, more evaporation occurs, so you will need extra stock.

Warm Cherries and Cream

This is one of my favorite quick desserts. Sexy and luscious, the cream swoons into the cherry sauce, mingling hot and cool and colors and textures.

¼ pound cherries, pitted
1 tablespoon honey or sugar
Squeeze of lemon juice
¼ cup crème fraîche or whipped cream
1 tablespoon grated dark chocolate (optional)

Place cherries in a small saucepan and heat them to a boil, mashing with a wooden spoon. Add honey or sugar, and continue to cook until the fruit begins to break down and gives off a jammy syrup. Cook another 2 to 3 minutes and remove from the heat. Add lemon juice.

Cool slightly, divide between two shallow bowls, and top with crème fraiche or whipped cream (and chocolate, if desired). Serve warm.

12

Breakfast Beginnings

Segue into breakfast. The rehearsal is over. You're comfy in your relationship, confident in your knowledge of each other's taste, it's morning, and you're ravenous. Also for some real breakfast. As the dough for the chocolate-cinnamon buns rises, you can keep yourself busy and come back to it when it's time to knead some more.

Pineapple and Raspberries

I think of pineapples and raspberries as the yin and yang of fruits: complemented by their shapes, flavors, degrees of acidity and sweetness. Together, they're the perfect combination.

½ perfectly ripe pineapple, peeled, cored, and diced into
    1-inch pieces
4 ounces fresh raspberries, washed and dried
2 teaspoons lime juice
1 tablespoon honey, melted

Combine fruit, taking care not to break the raspberries. Add the lime juice and honey and stir to coat.

> *I have perfumed my bed with myrrh, aloes and cinnamon. Come let us take our fill of love.*
>
> —Proverbs 7:17–18

Chocolate-Cinnamon Breakfast Buns

What's sexier than homemade breakfast buns? Kneading dough? Of all the rhythms in the kitchen, the slow and steady pushing and pulling back and forth of dough is surely one of the most suggestive. When you're comfortable enough to start making something together, to "proof" the relationship, bread is the perfect candidate.

First, get started on the dough. Kneading can get messy, so maybe you want to do that in the buff. Get a little playful and daub each other with some dough, then wash it off in the shower while the dough's rising . . .

Now add cinnamon to the mix, considered a potent aphrodisiac for millennia, and your kitchen's going to heat up! Surveys show that when it comes to aromas that induce male excitation, cinnamon heads the list.

Who better to inspire your breakfast fixings than Norman Love (who makes a wicked cinnamon-chocolate beignet) and "The Naked Chef" Jamie Oliver (who bakes a delicious chocolate twister bread)? This recipe was influenced by the breakfast treats of those chefs. Because these cinnamon buns are made from bread dough, they need time to rise, so wait until you have a leisurely weekend morning to make them. You first make a basic bread recipe, then finish it up with cinnamon and chocolate and roll it into buns.

You'll have enough buns for several days. Wrap the other half of the dough tightly and put it in the refrigerator for up to 4 days, until you're ready to bake it.

1 ounce fresh cake yeast or 3 packages (¼ ounce each) active dry yeast

2 tablespoons honey or sugar

3 cups tepid water plus a little extra

2 pounds (6 to 8 cups) bread flour plus a little extra

2 tablespoons salt

¾ cup plus 2 tablespoons soft butter

7 ounces walnuts or pecans, lightly toasted and crushed or broken up

1 teaspoon cinnamon

11 ounces semisweet or bittersweet (70%) chocolate, best quality you can afford, chopped or grated

Dissolve the yeast and honey or sugar in half the tepid water. On a clean surface or in a large bowl, make a pile of the flour and salt. Make a well in the center and pour in all the dissolved yeast mixture. Using one hand, slowly incorporate the flour, moving from the center and out, until all the yeast mixture is absorbed. Then pour the other half of the tepid water into the center and gradually add all the flour to make a moist dough. (Some flours may need a little more water, so feel free to adjust quantities.)

Kneading! Roll, push, and fold the dough over, repeat; knead for 5 minutes. This develops the gluten and the structure of the dough, your arm muscles, and your sex appeal. If any of the dough sticks to your hands, add more flour to them. Flour both your hands well, and lightly flour the top of the dough. Make it into a round, high shape, and place it on a baking tray. Deeply score the dough with a knife.

Leave it to rise until it's doubled in size. A warm, moist, draft-free place such as near a warm stove provides the quickest rise, but you don't want it to rise too quickly. If you have to, though, the dough can be covered with plastic wrap to speed things up. Depending on conditions, the rise takes about 40 minutes.

When the dough has doubled in size, punch it down. Shape it as you like—round or flat—and leave it to rise for a second time until it doubles in size.

Divide the dough into equal parts and refrigerate half. Preheat the oven to 400 degrees. Push the dough into a square shape on a floured board, then roll it out on all sides until it is a long rectangle about 7 inches wide and ¼ inch thick. Using a pastry brush or knife, spread the butter thinly across the dough. Sprinkle over the nuts, the cinnamon, then the chocolate, and roll up across the width like a jelly roll. Cut into 1-inch-thick slices.

Place the slices next to each other on a greased baking sheet, cut-side upward, with a little space in between. Bake for around 20 minutes. Cool for 20 minutes before eating.

Dulce de Leche

Dulce de Leche is really just Mexican caramel, as innocent as the Italian Nutella, but with a name as exotic and va-va-voom as that of an X-rated film star. It's the ultimate spread.

If you want the Dulce de Leche for breakfast, make it a day or two ahead in order to allow for the chill time. It's delicious with the Chocolate-Cinnamon Breakfast Buns and also very good with bread pudding, ice cream, or crepes.

> 1½ cups sugar
> 2 cups whole milk
> ⅛ teaspoon baking soda
> 2 cups goat's milk or regular whole milk

Put the sugar in a heavy saucepan and pour in the 2 cups of whole milk. Cook over medium heat until the mixture comes to a boil, 10 to 15 minutes. Reduce the heat to low and simmer without stirring until the color changes to a light brown caramel color, 15 to 20 minutes. To check color, remove the pan from the burner and allow to cool about 10 seconds, then stir carefully; the mixture will foam up but will soon subside and the color will be easier to see. When it has achieved the desired shade of brown, allow the mixture to rest.

In a separate small saucepan, heat the baking soda with the goat's milk over low heat. Bring to a boil, which will take about

15 minutes. Carefully stir the goat's milk mixture into the caramel-ized milk.

Return the saucepan to the burner and continue to simmer carefully, checking periodically, until the mixture coats the back of a spoon. This takes about 2½ hours. Allow the Dulche de Leche to cool, then store it in a glass jar in the refrigerator for at least 2½ to 3 hours before using.

Scrambled Eggs and Bacon

The egg is perhaps the ultimate example of the dichotomy of complexity and simplicity. Considered a source of sexual vitality and the most popular (and obvious) reproductive symbol, eggs embody procreation. In the Greek Orthodox tradition, as well as in Chinese, Arab, and Indian cultures, the egg reigns supreme as a symbol of rejuvenation. The last chapter of the seduction manual The Perfumed Garden *is entitled "Forming the Conclusion of This Work, and Treating of the Good Effects of the Deglutition of Eggs as Favorable to the Coitus." In the Japanese film* Tampopo, *two lovers pass a raw, quivering egg yolk back and forth between each other's mouths, until it nearly bursts.*

What better way to celebrate a late morning in bed than serving your lover the ultimate yin and yang, male and female, bacon and eggs? These eggs are divinely rich and creamy. The recipe comes from friends who were on their honeymoon in Australia and discovered a delightful little restaurant famous for its eggs. My friend told me, "I thought I'd died and gone to heaven last night—these eggs made me think again!" Her husband giggled.

    4 slices Danish bacon
    1½ teaspoons butter
    6 eggs
    ½ cup cream or half-and-half
    Salt and pepper

Place the bacon in a frying or sauté pan and fry until crisp. Drain on paper towels.

When the bacon is nearly cooked, melt the butter over medium heat in a medium–size nonstick frying or sauté pan. Whisk together the eggs, cream, salt, and pepper. Add mixture to the pan with the melted butter and let set for 15 to 20 seconds before stirring. Stir slowly with a wooden spoon, pushing and folding the eggs in from the rim to the center. Let set again for another 15 to 20 seconds and repeat the stirring process. Remove the pan from the heat and let the eggs finish cooking, then stir once more.

Serve the eggs with the bacon.

> *They dined on mince and slices of quince,*
> *Which they ate with a runcible spoon;*
> *And hand in hand, on the edge of the sand,*
> *They danced by the light of the moon.*
>
> —Edward Lear, *The Owl and the Pussy-Cat*

Tartine with Quince Jam

Native to Persia, quinces crop up in all kinds of ancient tomes. Many scholars believe Eve tempted Adam with a quince, not an apple, nor the fig, in the Garden of Eden. Pliny writes about the fruit's medicinal virtues; its color, many seeds, and aromas inform the Greek references to quince and Aphrodite. Romans associated quinces with the Goddess of Beauty, Venus, making the fruit the symbol of love and happiness and a good omen for conjugal union.

Quinces are highly fragrant, they cook up a lovely red color, and are also delicious made as a jam, with or without apples. The French add a few drops of rosewater and a few drops of musk to their quince jam. Called continiat, it is considered a digestivo and an aphrodisiac.

If you cannot find fresh quinces for the following recipe, you may also be able to find quince jam through a specialty supplier or market and dress it up with lemon zest. If unavailable, substitute another type of fruit jam.

Tartine is the most popular French breakfast. From the French tartiner (to spread), it refers to a piece of bread and just about anything sweet or savory you spread on top of it—jam, chocolate, cheese. Varied types of preserves are served on tartine at my favorite downtown New York bistro, Les Deux Gamins, a hip, fun little place employing some of the friendliest waitresses in town.

You can make your own bread using the leftover bread dough from the Chocolate-Cinnamon Breakfast Buns, or you can just buy the best French baguette you can find.

 1 pound quinces
 1 tablespoon minced fresh ginger
 1 pound sugar
 8 ounces water
 Baguette or other bread

To make quince jam, pare and core the quinces. Put them with the ginger in a medium–size pan. Add the sugar and water. Bring to a boil and simmer until soft and just beginning to turn red, about 10 minutes.

Cool, mash with a spoon, and push through a sieve if you like a smoother and less chunky jam.

Spread on the baguette and enjoy. Any leftover jam can be stored in refrigerator for up to 1 week.

Culinary Quickie

Honey

A richly erudite and complex woman I know, a professor studying to be an Oriba priestess, tells me that honey has the "Love Voodoo." Oriba is a sect of the West African Yoruba people, and honey is the attribute of Oshun (also spelled Oxum and Osun), a Yoruban goddess of sexual love and money, who specializes in sensual delights. All recipes that use honey belong to her, and honey can be used in many ways to "sweeten" people up, in addition to its many powerful ancient associations.

Honey is the most perfect carbohydrate known to humans. The simple sugars it contains perfectly agree with our body chemistry, and its chemical makeup is such that our body absorbs it into our bloodstream nearly effortlessly. Use it liberally in your recipes and love potions.

Resources

This is a highly subjective list of resources for food and cookware.

Adriana's Caravan
www.adrianascaravan.com
800–316–0820

Great source for a wide array of culinary exotica, herbs, spices, oils, and vinegars. They also have a retail outlet in New York's Grand Central Terminal.

Bueno Foods
www.buenofoods.com
800–95–CHILE

Fresh New Mexico chiles in season, frozen chopped chiles, chile powders, and puree.

The Chile Shop
www.thechileshop.com
505–983–6080

Great selection of dried chiles and chile powder and blue-corn products.

Esperya
www.esperya.com/usa
877–907–2525

Good source for hard-to-find Italian products, including cheese, honey, books, even seafood.

The Ethnic Grocer
www.ethnicgrocer.com
866–438–4642

Good source for pestos, pastes, chutneys, spices, and sauces, along with recipes and cooking tips.

Kalustyans
www.kalustyans.com
212–685–3451

Beans, breads, essences, grains, lentils, dals, nuts, olives, pomegranate molasses, Turkish red pepper paste, rices, spices, and coarse semolina.

Melissa's Specialty Foods
www.melissas.com
800–588–0151
Corn husks, spices, pepper jellies, salsas.

The Mozzarella Company
www.mozzco.com
800–798–2954
Excellent specialty Italian and Mexican cheeses.

Neal's Yard
www.nyr-usa.com
999–697–8721
Founded twenty years ago from the original Neal's Yard in London's Covent Garden, famous for its herbals and botanicals, cheese and bread, Neal's Yard products are now available in the United States. Their essential oils are some of the finest made.

The New Cooks' Catalogue
Knopf, 2000
This updated book is an indispensable guide to every piece of kitchen equipment you can imagine and a great reference tool to peruse before starting to shop.

The Rare Wine Company
www.rarewineco.com
800–999–4342

Excellent source for rare wines as well as the finest balsamic vinegars and olive oils.

The Spanish Table
www.tablespan.com
Seattle, WA: 206–682–2927
Berkeley, CA: 510–548–1383
Santa Fe, NM: 505–986–0243
An excellent repertoire of the best of Spain: olive oils, olives, herbs, honeys, kitchen utensils, books, CDs, and wines.

The Spice House
www.thespicehouse.com
847–328–3711
Good source and great selection of high-quality spices and herbs.

Western Date Ranches
www.medjooldates.com
928–726 7006
Great source for dates and organic dates.

Zingerman's Delicatessen
www.zingermans.com
313–662–DELI
Balsamic vinegars, olive oil, cheeses, and chocolates.

Index